A COMMUNITY OF BELIEVERS

Making Church Membership More Meaningful

Charles W. Deweese

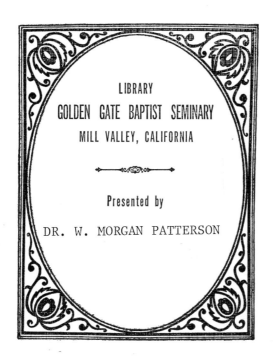

Judson Press ® Valley Forge

A COMMUNITY OF BELIEVERS

Library of Congress Cataloging in Publication Data

Deweese. Charles W
  A community of believers.

  Includes bibliographical references.
  1. Baptists—Membership. 2. Baptists—Doctrinal and controversial works—Baptist authors. 3. Church discipline. 4. Covenants (Church polity) I. Title.
BX6331.2.D48   262'.06'1   77-16687
ISBN 0-8170-0755-5

To

my mother
Faye Warren Deweese
(1925-1961)

and

my father
James Philip Deweese
(1922-)

who taught me that church membership
means responsibility

Preface

Central to the Baptist view of the church is an emphasis on a regenerate church membership. Unfortunately, trends away from a regenerate membership are all too clear in contemporary Baptist life. These trends include an increase in the evangelizing and baptizing of young children, a rise in the number of nonresident church members, a swelling of the number of inactive resident members, a careless approach to basic membership duties and practices, and a decline of the ethical standards of many members.

The purposes of this book are: (1) to describe the inconsistencies between actual Baptist practices and the historic Baptist doctrine of a regenerate church membership, and (2) to present positive and practical guidelines designed to help Baptists reaffirm and implement in their churches the regenerate intentions of the New Testament and Baptist history. It is hoped that pastors and the laity will find this work a useful tool for raising the regenerate status of their churches. The quality of our Baptist future depends, in some respects, upon the achievement of this goal.

The ideas for this volume began to take shape in 1972 when the Historical Commission of the Southern Baptist Convention gave to me the Davis C. Woolley Award for the Study of Church

Covenants. This money made easier the preparation of a Ph.D. dissertation, "The Origin, Development, and Use of Church Covenants in Baptist History," completed in 1973 at the Southern Baptist Theological Seminary in Louisville, Kentucky. (Some of the material in this book is adapted from the dissertation.) Further development of the ideas occurred from 1974 to 1976 through the writing of several articles and curriculum units for publications of the Historical Commission and Sunday School Board of the Southern Baptist Convention.

Special appreciation goes to six persons. W. Morgan Patterson, presently Dean of Academic Affairs at Golden Gate Baptist Theological Seminary in Mill Valley, California, cultivated my initial interest in Baptist church covenants while director of my graduate program at Southern Seminary. James Leo Garrett, Jr., presently Director of the J. M. Dawson Church-State Studies at Baylor University in Waco, Texas, supervised my dissertation and expanded my interest in a regenerate church membership. Lynn E. May, Jr., Executive Director of the Historical Commission of the Southern Baptist Convention, has given valuable encouragement, as my employer, for me to do this writing. Harold L. Twiss, Managing Editor of Judson Press, has been sensitive to the issues at stake in this volume and has related as a friend. Most important, Mary Jane and Dana, my wife and child, have relinquished lots of family time in order for this ministry to be possible. I am grateful for their support.

Charles W. Deweese

Contents

1
Maintaining a Regenerate Church Membership

Modern Baptists are continually tempted to accommodate themselves to the enticements of American culture and to abandon essential religious commitments. Ethical compromises, spiritual convenience, church attendance with minimal involvement, an occasional nod to God, the spectator syndrome, and the view of God and the church as optional are characteristic of a fairly common approach to church membership. A strikingly clear example of unfulfilled commitments resides in the nonresident membership problem. Nonresident members account for about 20 percent of the total membership of the American Baptist Churches in the U.S.A. and for over 25 percent of the total membership of the Southern Baptist Convention. The sad point is that almost four million American and Southern Baptists have virtually no relationship with the churches of their membership.

The nonresident membership problem reflects the failure of Baptists to join new churches when they move to new communities. It also reflects two failures of Baptist churches. One is inadequate education concerning church membership obligations, and the other is the widespread absence of responsible ministries to members who have moved away. When a young person leaves home to attend college in another city, Christian parents do not cease to care for and support that child. Family encouragement remains constant. That a Baptist church will often cease to care for and support members of its spiritual family who move to new residences is a strange turn of events.

To speak of American Baptists as being about 1,600,000 strong and of Southern Baptists as being about 13,000,000 strong is to employ bragging statistics that inflate the truth. Only after subtracting large numbers of members unaccounted for does the resident membership come into focus. The problem of uncommitted membership does not stop here, for not all resident members engage actively in church affairs. In the American Baptist Churches in the U.S.A., less than 50 percent of the resident members are enrolled in Sunday schools.[1] In the Southern Baptist Convention, slightly less than 80 percent of the resident members are enrolled in Sunday schools.[2] To take the percentages and level of commitment down even further, many of those enrolled in Sunday schools do not attend regularly, and many who do attend are visitors and children who are not church members.

Another primary membership duty often neglected is that of contributing financially to the church and God's work. The per capita contributions of American Baptists in 1975 was $110.63 and that of Southern Baptists was $115.84. This ranked the former forty-first and the latter fortieth in a list of forty-two denominational bodies.[3] By contrast, the per capita gross income in 1975 of all persons living in Texas, North Carolina, New York, and Oregon was, respectively, $5,631, $4,952, $6,564, and $5,769.[4] A tithe to the churches by the Baptists in any of these states would have exceeded by four times the per capita contributions actually made. Does the percentage of the income given to God by Baptists through their churches have any direct relationship with spiritual responsibility? The claim of 1 Timothy 6:10 that "the love of money is the root of all evils" suggests that the answer is yes.

Further, the failure to meet membership duties is visible in the breakdown of the ethical standards of church members. The involvement of Christians in the drug culture, in alcoholic beverage consumption, in sexual deviations, in the proliferation of divorces, in pornography, in manipulative business practices, as well as other questionable pursuits, is plain evidence of the gradual weakening of a regenerate church membership. Moral absolutes and related responsibilities are being displaced by moral relativities and deteriorating spiritual commitments. Viable steps must be taken to reverse this trend by instructing church members in the fundamentals of biblical ethics, by addressing the Bible to contemporary moral concerns, and by disciplining members who refuse to hear and heed the ethical teachings of the church.

What approaches can Baptists take to resolve the tension between the biblical ideal of a regenerate church membership and current patterns toward a nonregenerate membership? The answer to that question is what this book is all about. Let me quickly state my belief that the issue at stake is immensely important to the quality of Baptist life and deserves urgent consideration. Baptists will do well to apply some of their best thinking to the tasks of accenting the positive values of a regenerate church membership, exposing superficial trends which abandon the biblical content of this doctrine, and presenting creative alternatives for counteracting decline in church membership commitment. Perhaps this book will help to encourage new insights in these areas.

REGENERATE CHURCH MEMBERSHIP DEFINED

The first task is to define a regenerate church membership. Alongside believer's baptism, congregational polity, the associational principle, and the separation of church and state, the concept of a regenerate church membership has always been a distinguishing mark of Baptists and has permeated historical Baptist teachings on the nature of the church.[5] Although the idea of a regenerate church membership existed in Protestantism prior to the rise of Baptists in early seventeenth-century England, Baptists have led the way in contributing the doctrine to Protestant growth.[6]

What is regeneration? After reviewing the New Testament evidence, one scholar defined the term "as a drastic act on fallen human nature by the Holy Spirit, leading to a change in the person's whole outlook. He can now be described as a new man who seeks, finds, and follows God in Christ."[7] This suggests that the initiative for regeneration comes from God and is not derived from human effort. God "saved us, not because of deeds done by us in righteousness, but in virtue of his own mercy, by the washing of regeneration and renewal in the Holy Spirit" (Titus 3:5).

Who are the regenerate? These are persons who have received

new birth from the Holy Spirit. This new birth can be understood only in the context of human sin and God's salvation. Jesus stated in his encounter with Nicodemus that "unless one is born of water and the Spirit, he cannot enter the kingdom of God" (John 3:5). A regenerate person is one who repents of sin, commits one's life to God in Christ through public profession of faith, and applies this commitment in daily living. Although he or she is not perfect, the person born of God ideally "does right," "loves," "overcomes the world," and "does not sin" (1 John 2:29; 4:7; 5:4, 18). "The regenerate man walks after the Spirit, lives in the Spirit, is led by the Spirit, and is commanded to be filled with the Spirit."[8]

What is the relationship between the regenerate person and church membership? From the Baptist perspective, only the regenerate can be legitimate members of a New Testament church. If a church is comprised mainly of the nonregenerate, it can become a social and secular body with few spiritual distinctives. Having lost its sense of being set apart by God for a special mission, such a church neutralizes its witness, renders an empty ministry, and negates whatever moral and spiritual impact it might be able to have on the world. The church is not intended to be a worldly organization. To be in the world in active witness and ministry, but not of the world, is the ideal for the church.

Definitions of the church which have appeared in Baptist confessions of faith throughout the centuries clarify the perpetual Baptist stress on a regenerate church membership. In 1611, Thomas Helwys, soon to become the pastor of the first Baptist congregation in England, wrote a statement of faith, which became the first English Baptist confession, in which he described the church as a company of faithful Christians who have separated from the world, confessed their sins, acknowledged their faith in God, and knit themselves to God and one another by baptism.[9] These same elements characterize descriptions of the church found in practically all Baptist confessions of faith.[10] The combined thrust of these definitions of the church is that the regenerate can fulfill their response to God only within the context of the church, and the church can achieve its mission for God only if comprised of the regenerate.

Regeneration can be a required condition for church membership only in a country where there is no state church. When a church consists by political and ecclesiastical mandate of all the people born in a particular geographical area, church membership becomes equivalent to national citizenship. In such a situation the church is not comprised of gathered believers, but rather of involuntary participants who may or may not be regenerated by the Holy Spirit. This is a key reason why Baptists place heavy emphasis on the maintenance of religious liberty and the separation of church and state. John Clarke, Isaac Backus, John Leland, and, for a short time, Roger Williams were among the multitudes of Baptist leaders in early America who sought to saturate the American dream with these cherished concepts.

Their doctrine of a regenerate church membership compelled early Baptists to fight for religious liberty. A regenerate church membership could be a reality only in a national and religious climate which did not force all citizens, regenerate and nonregenerate, into a common church. Religious liberty and the separation of church and state would allow both the voluntary aspect of church membership and the requirement that every member be a baptized believer to function apart from any outside intervention. Thus, religious liberty and a regenerate church membership are kinsmen.

A direct relationship exists between a regenerate church membership and five other areas of Baptist life—church covenants, the ordinances, church discipline, evangelism, and small groups. Subsequent chapters will attempt to show how innovative practices in these five areas can improve the regenerate qualities of Baptist churches. For the present it is sufficient to say that believer's baptism, as the mark of entrance into the church, is an important safeguard which enables a regenerate church membership to become a reality. Baptist confessions of faith are at one in stressing the centrality of believer's baptism in creating a regenerate church membership.[11] If believer's baptism is the safeguard for the rise of a regenerate church membership, the regular celebration of the Lord's Supper is a safeguard for the preservation of regenerate congregations. Baptist statements of faith have announced in unison through the ages that only Christian believers who have been baptized can properly partake of the Lord's Supper. Restraints against participation by the nonregenerate are loud and clear.[12] Statements of faith have also claimed that the concept of a regenerate church membership includes covenantal pledges which regenerate members make to God and to fellow church members,[13] church discipline which regenerate congregations administer redemptively,[14] and evangelistic witness which all the regenerate share.[15] Further, Baptist experience in the past has demonstrated that small groups within churches must exhibit regenerate features.

TRENDS TOWARD A NONREGENERATE MEMBERSHIP

Baptists face a basic contradiction at the heart of their approach to a regenerate church membership. The documents of our faith make clear that this doctrine is crucial to a proper understanding of individual discipleship and of institutional church life. Yet many membership practices offer plain evidence that the doctrine is all too frequently taken lightly and, in some instances, treated with "a grain of salt." In addition to the nonresident membership problem and other unfulfilled commitments already discussed, trends toward a nonregenerate membership among Baptists in America fall into at least three categories— weak baptismal and Lord's Supper practices, deviations from important historical Baptist practices, and the misuse of a Baptist doctrine. All these trends are creating destructive consequences for the concept of the church as consisting of baptized believers and committed practitioners. Baptists will do well to counter these trends with multiplied vigor. The first step in the encounter is simply to recognize the trends and their capacity to pulverize the key element in the Baptist concept of the church.

The first trend centers on problems relating to baptism and the Lord's Supper. These problems begin with the widespread absence of pre-baptismal training in Baptist life. Baptismal candidates are not sufficiently informed of the expectations which the church will have of them in the areas of doctrine and conduct. Rather, candidates are all too often hastened to the baptismal pool with the minister and congregation assuming in simplicity that immersion will insure integrity in doctrine and practice. Is it possible that churches do not believe it important to share their doctrinal and ethical expectations with baptismal candidates, or do many churches simply have no expectations for new members? Whatever the case, the result is that a church does injustice both to its new members by depriving them of essential knowledge in key biblical, historical, theological, and practical matters, and to itself by lowering the standards of entrance into its membership.

Another problem is the baptizing of children too young to make responsible spiritual decisions. Recently I talked to a preschool teacher from a Baptist church who was extremely concerned that her pastor had recently baptized several three-year-olds and that he regularly performed active evangelistic witness to preschoolers. Infant baptism is an absolute perversion of a regenerate church membership, but the momentum toward infant baptism is mounting. If this trend is not checked and even reversed, the traditional Baptist understanding of the church will be in jeopardy. One harsh evidence that many children are being baptized too young is the growing tendency for teenagers to request re-baptism. They claim that their first baptism was virtually meaningless because of their inability as small children to comprehend its significance.

One other apparent weakness in the baptismal practices of many churches is the tendency to treat the actual baptismal event too lightly. Many times baptisms are approached as if they are mere appendages to the "more important" parts of worship services, such as the preaching of the administrators. Further, the baptisms are frequently scheduled for Sunday night services when about one-third as many people are present as on Sunday morning. Baptism occurs once in the life of a Christian, represents one's initiation into church membership, and should not be a hurried affair. Each candidate for church membership deserves more than to be rushed through the baptismal waters in a thirty-second routine that is sometimes less than meaningful. Further, baptisms should take place when the largest number of members is present. If the total church supports each new member at baptism, then that new member will find it easier to fit into the patterns characterizing the total church as a regenerate fellowship. Lastly, worship services would do well to center around baptisms and not be encumbered by them. Baptism is not a peripheral experience for a new church member; it is integral to one's acceptance of new spiritual commitments and should be treated with dignity.

If three-year-olds are being baptized, then three-year-olds are participating in the Lord's Supper. When the depths of many of the theological themes surrounding the Lord's Supper often elude the understanding of even the most mature church members, is it fair to assume that a child just past babyhood in age can possess even a rudimentary grasp of the themes? Such themes as sacrifice, thanksgiving, covenant, and memorial, all of which (and more) fit into a healthy view of the Lord's Supper, are too difficult for the small child. If a child partakes of the Lord's Supper without any knowledge of the content of these themes, the ordinance is little more than a refreshment time for him. To administer the Supper to children just past infancy degrades the New Testament meaning of the event, places on the children a requirement they cannot meet, and encourages a nonregenerate membership.

Like baptism, the Lord's Supper celebration is often relegated to a worship setting in which only a small part of the congregation is present. The implications are that it is simply not convenient to serve the Supper to a larger body of church members or that the Supper is not important enough to consume the worship time of the larger body. Another possible explanation is that pastors run out of ways to make the Supper an exciting worship experience; so they shift the ordinance to a time slot in which fewer people will be exposed to their lack of preparation. Whatever the reason, the point is missed that the Lord's Supper is by New Testament example the worship experience par excellence. All members should be present at the Supper, and the Supper should be the worship service, rather than subsidiary to a sermon on a nonrelated subject.

A second trend toward a nonregenerate membership relates to departures from critically important historical Baptist practices. Three such practices abandoned far too widely include church covenants, church discipline, and authentic evangelism. In our Baptist past, covenants and discipline have been integral to the understanding of the church as regenerate. Covenants capsulized the disciplines (prayer, Bible study, regular attendance, ministries, small group work, and others) to which church members pledged themselves. Read frequently during celebrations of the Lord's Supper, on special covenant days, and at other occasions, covenants were taken seriously. The covenant-breaker became the subject of the discipline of a congregation. Granted, covenants and discipline were sometimes so legalistic and punitive in function that their weaknesses outweighed their values, but more often than not these features of church life helped insure the integrity of individual members and the corporate church. Covenants and discipline are largely absent from churches today, and this neglect is adding to the deterioration of a regenerate church membership.

In their obsession for visible success, many churches and church leaders are enamored by statistics and use a "superficial type of evangelism" in which "people are maneuvered into premature decisions" and "the methods of worldly salesmanship are utilized rather than depending on the presence and power of the divine Spirit."[16] Superficial evangelism, coupled with the casual way of voting members into churches, provides a good explanation for the high number of inactive church members.

Not only are certain techniques of evangelism at fault, but also the theology behind some evangelistic practices symbolizes the surrendering of a traditional and solidly biblical foundation for sharing the good news about Christ to non-Christians. Baptists have taught for centuries that it is necessary to seek repentance for sin only from those persons considered personally accountable for their spiritual conditions. The active evangelism by many Baptist pastors of preschoolers, who certainly cannot be placed by any biblical standard in the category of the accountable, raises some serious questions about the Baptist doctrine of evangelism. If the application of evangelism to preschoolers continues to grow, it will be to the obvious detriment of a regenerate church membership. When a major Baptist statement of faith asserts that "it is the duty of every child of God to seek constantly to win the lost to Christ,"[17] the implication is that those who are not lost do not need to be won. Preschoolers fit into the latter category, and Baptists need to harmonize contemporary evangelistic practices with their historical evangelistic doctrine.

Perhaps the greatest danger to a regenerate church membership which relates to evangelism is not bad techniques nor the evangelism of preschoolers but the failure of Baptists to engage in evangelism as a natural expression of their discipleship and churchmanship. Church members relegate evangelism to church staffs, and evangelism becomes the work of paid professionals. The voluntary element diminishes; the number of church members involved in evangelism grows smaller; and the tragic result is fewer new Christians. The regenerate church will activate its evangelistic witness and share it through the broad ranks of congregational life.

One last trend toward a nonregenerate membership relates to misuses of the Baptist doctrine of eternal security. This is a most acceptable doctrine when interpreted as God's guarantee of salvation for that person who has an initial experience of regeneration and subsequent and progressive experiences of sanctification. A problem erupts for a regenerate church member-ship when members use this doctrine, either deliberately or subconsciously, to justify or rationalize less than Christian conduct. "If God once saved me," so the deceptive logic goes, "then it really does not matter how I live my life." But the logic forgets that salvation is a continuous process and that responsible Christian action and works are essential in expressing the impact which the salvation of God is exerting on one's life. The question may also need to be raised as to whether members who misuse the Baptist doctrine in question have indeed experienced the regeneration of the Holy Spirit.

A dilemma facing contemporary Baptists in America is how to reconcile mounting trends toward an uncommitted nonregenerate membership with doctrinal statements which require a committed regenerate membership. Baptists advocate believer's baptism but baptize three-year-olds. Baptists include covenantal themes in their definitions of the church but generally fail to write and implement church covenants. Baptists recognize the value of discipline in individual, family, and civil life but largely fail to activate it in church life. Baptists stress the importance of sharing the good news of Jesus Christ to non-Christians but often deny themselves the privilege by assigning this task to professional members of church staffs.

An English Baptist confession of faith stated over 285 years ago that "the purest Churches under heaven are subject to mixture, and error."[18] In trying to achieve a regenerate church membership, early English Baptists sought "not a sinless community, but a committed community."[19] To gain and retain a committed community, these and later Baptists stressed, among other things, church covenants, believer's baptism, the Lord's Supper, church discipline, authentic evangelism, and the integrity of small groups within churches. Since no one can deny that there are weaknesses in the current Baptist understanding and application of a regenerate church membership, it seems perfectly in order to take a new and innovative look at these historical Baptist emphases. The remaining chapters will offer some positive and practical suggestions designed to help churches strengthen their regenerate character and sharpen the moral and spiritual integrity of each member. The goal is to encourage deeper attachment to New Testament principles of church membership.

2

Church Membership in Covenant

A church covenant creatively written and carefully imple-
mented can be one of the finest tools available enabling a Baptist
church to acquire and maintain a regenerate church membership.
Church covenants have been a feature of Baptist life since the 1600s
and have regularly given a boost to the regenerate ideal of the
church when responsibly used. Although early Baptists in America
assigned much importance to church covenants, Baptists of the
twentieth century have largely neglected them. This neglect
prompted the recent claim: "Few people know the significance of
the covenant idea in the history of their churches, and little attempt
is made to impress upon them the significance of their words when
they read this document together."[1] This claim is both accurate
and disturbing. Perhaps this chapter can provide a sound basis for
recovering the strengths intrinsic to a healthy approach to church
covenants.

A church covenant is a series of pledges which church members
voluntarily make to God and one another. These vows reflect
biblically based guidelines by which church members intend to
conduct themselves or practice their faith as Christians. Whereas a
confession of faith focuses on doctrine, a church covenant centers

19

on conduct. The ethical dimension of the Christian life is prominent in covenantal promises.

The major confessions of faith of Baptists in America have clearly identified covenanting as integral to the nature of the church. Consistency between faith and action creates two options for Baptists. We can either eliminate the covenantal emphasis from our affirmations about the church and abandon covenanting, or we can take seriously the covenantal commitments which are inherent in our understanding of the church. Selection of the former option will run counter to traditional Baptist practice, at least as it existed in the seventeenth through much of the nineteenth centuries. Selection of the latter option will add substance to the Baptist doctrine of the church. If Baptists believe that covenantal themes are so vital in defining a church, then the achievement of consonance between faith and practice demands a new devotion to covenantal pledges.

UNDERSTANDING CHURCH COVENANTS

Why should Baptists use church covenants? What are the positive values which can emerge from their use? The answers to these questions are basic to the practical suggestions for writing and implementing covenants which comprise the latter two-thirds of this chapter. Further, the reader will find a knowledge of the reasons for and values of church covenants to be a helpful prologue to the entire book, for the covenantal theme will manifest itself in every chapter.

1. The first reason why Baptists should be a covenanting people is that covenanting has a biblical basis. Old Testament people frequently bound themselves to God and one another with covenants. Josiah covenanted "to walk after the Lord and to keep his commandments and his testimonies and his statutes, with all his heart and all his soul, to perform the words of this covenant that were written in this book; and all the people joined in the covenant" (2 Kings 23:3). The people under the governorship of Nehemiah prepared a covenant, wrote it down, and had it sealed by their princes, Levites, and priests (Nehemiah 9:38). They pledged to follow the law given to Moses by God, and they specified other obligations to which they devoted themselves, most of which dealt with supporting God's house (Nehemiah 10:30-39). Even the Dead Sea Scrolls made much of the covenant idea. Initiation into the

Qumran community required a covenant of dedication by each new member that he would obey the Mosaic law.[2]

Covenantal pledges of the New Testament find expression in baptism, the Lord's Supper, church discipline, and in passages on various other subjects. These covenantal relationships will be exhibited in subsequent chapters. For now, let us look at a separate New Testament motif which has obvious covenantal implications. This is the motif of the church as the Bride of Christ (see, for example, Ephesians 5:32; Revelation 21:9; 22:17). If we compare the ideal relationship between Christ and the church to the model of an ideal human marriage, we quickly recognize the need for the church to become one with Christ in mutual compact. Following the lead already established by Christ, the church develops a sense of reciprocal sacrifice, cultivates shared love for Christ and his causes, and deepens dialogue with him. Since "Christ loved the church and gave himself up for her," the church as the Bride of Christ must recognize that "Christ is the head of the church, his body, and is himself its Savior" and that "the church is subject to Christ" (Ephesians 5:23-25). These words of the apostle Paul place the church in an undeniable context of covenant. Most important, they demonstrate that the covenant has a dimension of ultimate consequence for the church.

2. Covenanting is theologically sound. We must covenant with God because God has covenanted with us. Biblical theology is saturated with covenants evolving from God's initiative. God covenanted, for example, with Noah (Genesis 6:18; 9:8-17), Abraham (Genesis 12:1-3; 15:18; 17:1-21), and David (2 Samuel 7:8-29; 23:5; 2 Chronicles 13:5; Psalm 89:3-4, 20-37). God offered a new covenant for Israel and Judah (Jeremiah 31:31-34). Christ mediated the new covenant by providing redemption for all who had transgressed under the old covenant. The new covenant was confirmed in the blood of Christ (Matthew 26:28).

A wise response to the personal pledges of God to the church is for the church to declare its allegiance to God. A primary reason for writing and using church covenants is that they give Baptists one way to make their expression of loyalty to God a continuing reality. Grounded in the covenantal agreements which God first confirmed by the gifts of creation and salvation, covenantal vows of faith and consecration are efforts by church members to respond to the graciousness of God. The theology behind a Baptist church covenant is that God's initiative in our favor demands our initiative in God's favor. A regenerate church membership can approximate fruition only when church members take seriously their covenantal assignments which are rooted in the Bible.

3. Covenanting has wide historical precedents among Baptists.[3] Seventeenth-century English Baptists used covenants extensively, as did the early Baptists in America. At least four features characterized the Baptist approach to covenants in the pre-1830 period in America. Churches tended to write individual covenants. Covenants were designed to meet the specific needs of local churches. Churches used covenants in multiple settings, such as baptism, the Lord's Supper, and the constituting of new churches. Church covenants and church discipline had a close relationship.

A trend toward uniformity has characterized covenantal usage since about 1830. J. Newton Brown, editorial secretary of the American Baptist Publication Society, published a covenant in 1853 (see Appendix A) which became and still is the most widely used single covenant among Baptists in the United States. Brown's covenant was actually his personal revision of the covenant initially published in 1833 by the New Hampshire Baptist Convention in conjunction with the New Hampshire Confession of Faith. At least four factors caused Brown's covenant to have an enormous circulation. First, it had a strong identification with the publication facilities of the American Baptist Publication Society. Second, it was included as a model covenant in many Baptist church manuals of the nineteenth and twentieth centuries. Third, the Landmark Baptists, who have greatly influenced Southern Baptists in concepts of the church, approved and sponsored this covenant. Fourth, the Sunday School Board of the Southern Baptist Convention tacitly accepted this covenant and distributed it widely in various types of literature and on small cards.

4. Many positive and practical values can emerge from a responsible use of church covenants. To begin with, they can help preserve a regenerate church membership by counteracting the situation in which an alarmingly high number of nonresident Baptists are only nominally related to local churches. In dealing with this very condition, one writer asserted that "the absence in some churches of any serious doctrinal or ethical standards for membership has cheapened the meaning of church member-ship."[4] It is precisely at the point of highlighting "ethical

standards for membership" that a church covenant can assume merit. Concerned with the conduct of a congregation and the way that its members practice their faith, a covenant accents ethical teachings of the Bible. A covenant does not create ethical standards and obligations; it condenses and reflects ethical duties which are biblical in origin. As a constant reminder of members' ethical responsibilities, a church covenant can function well in serving to alleviate the nonresident problem.

Another value from using a covenant, which is related to the first, is that faithful adherence to its contents can exert an influential role in the creation and maintenance of a disciplined church membership. To worship God and study the Bible regularly, to serve Christ consistently, to live ethically under the lordship of Christ, and to witness compassionately are among the disciplines which should comprise the substance of a covenant between the Christian, Christ, and fellow Christians.[5] Loyal devotion to these kinds of disciplines which form the heart of a covenant can considerably enhance the moral and spiritual progress and integrity of a congregation.

Church covenants can also be instruments for deepening the quality of fellowship in congregations. A genuine sense of Christian community can arise in churches as individual Baptists voluntarily verbalize their mutual commitments to God and one another. The underpinning of this covenantal togetherness is the awareness that all church members are equal in God's eyes, that all share in seeking common objectives, and that all are children of God. If used as a tool for growth, a church covenant can solidify a congregation around a mutual attachment to biblical obligations. The collective pledge to fulfill these duties helps to mold a church into the true family of God.

Covenantal experiences are one means by which Baptists can closely identify with the historical people of God and the cherished biblical disciplines which they taught and lived. Biblical personalities and the Christians of church history viewed covenanting as an essential expression of their faith. Baptists preserve the historical continuity of God's covenanters through participation in contemporary pledges.

Proper use of a covenant can lead a church to a keener understanding of its vital commitments. The spiritual and ethical expectations a church has of its members can become sharper.

Standards for the Christian growth of church members can become clarified. A covenant can stimulate regular evaluation of Christian maturation and church membership. It can establish a sense of dedication to a common set of goals and responsibilities. It can accent preventive discipline and thus preclude the necessity of corrective discipline. Adherence to a strong covenant can enhance the loyalty which members have to their church. Covenants have an instructional value in teaching new members features of Christian conduct considered to be of paramount importance. The tasks related to mature church membership receive more adequate magnification through serious covenanting. In none of the preceding values does a covenant supplant the Bible; rather, it simply elevates biblical principles to a conspicuous position in the life of church members.

Does a Baptist church actually have the right to expect a certain ethical life-style and standard of conduct from its members? A church built on the concept of a regenerate church membership has no alternative but to respond "yes." Further, such an expectation is more than a right; it is a duty. Many churches tragically fail to activate this expectation. A church covenant can become operative just at this point. Through a covenant a church can formulate its expectations. The result is more careful attention to the requirements for church membership. This new attention will cause each member to think more earnestly about the fundamentals of church membership.

WRITING CHURCH COVENANTS

Far and away the best procedure is for each Baptist church to write its own covenant, rather than appropriate one from some external source. There are disadvantages in using a prepared covenant, and there are several values associated with writing an individual and unique covenant. These disadvantages and values require some consideration here. Then will follow a systematic, step-by-step procedure a church can use in designing its personal covenantal statement.

Despite the prevailing practice of Baptist churches in early America to write separate covenants, the current pattern is for churches to adopt a prepared covenant, particularly the one published by J. Newton Brown in 1853. This latter approach has three liabilities which must be revealed and counteracted.

First, the widespread adoption of a standard covenant can contribute to a depreciation of covenantal interest and commitment. This has been the unexpected and paradoxical effect of printing uniform covenants in church manuals since the middle of the nineteenth century. With the appearance of the manuals, churches tended simply to adopt the covenants printed in them rather than write their own. As early as the turn of the century, one observer noted that with the use of these manuals, "the value of the church covenant has greatly deteriorated."[6]

The trend to accept uniform covenants has possibly represented a misunderstanding of Baptist polity and practice according to which each church has complete liberty to draw up its own covenant. The trend more probably reflects an ecclesiastical laziness. Churches have found it easier and more convenient to neglect the covenant idea or to adopt a uniform covenant than to engage in the work and discipline required to write their own. Church manuals and other literature which have sponsored specific covenants have contributed to the weakening of congregational discipline by making it unnecessary for churches to think through, struggle with, and write down the covenantal responsibilities to which they are willing to pledge themselves.

A second disadvantage, related especially to the broad use of J. Newton Brown's covenant, is that this covenant has several weaknesses. For one thing, it uses nineteenth-century words, such as "circumspectly" and "deportment," which have an antiquarian quality. The ambiguous clause "to religiously educate our children" could more appropriately be worded "to educate our children in the Christian faith."[7] Further, the covenant fails to make explicit that its promises are made to God as well as to fellow church members. This omission weakens the required theological thrust of a biblically based covenant.

Perhaps the most powerful indictment to be made against Brown's covenant is the uneven attention it gives to crucial social issues. The covenant gives a prominent position to an abhorrence of "the sale and use of intoxicating drinks," but it makes no reference to other social matters, such as drugs, pornography, economics, politics, and race (in recent appearances in the literature of the Sunday School Board of the Southern Baptist Convention, Brown's covenant has been revised to include statements on drugs and pornography). Thus the covenant does not provide guidance for Christian conduct in terms of some of the basic problems of contemporary times. Two options seem to be in order for writing a covenant. One is to list all the social ailments to which a covenant might address itself. The other is not to list the individual ethical issues but rather to state general and key principles which can be adapted to virtually any social involvement. The latter approach seems superior. Appendix B is an example of a covenant centering on biblical principles.

The third disadvantage related to the widespread publication and use of uniform covenants is the resulting tendency of Baptists to ascribe too much authority to them. The inclusion of J. Newton Brown's covenant in hundreds of thousands of copies of church manuals, hymnals, and periodicals was destined to magnify the authority of the covenant out of proportion. This tacit acceptance of a particular covenant by Baptist publishers has caused many Baptists to believe there is an official covenant for Baptist use. Such is not the case. A covenant has authority only when a church votes to give it authority. Model covenants printed in Baptist literature deserve no special prestige or status. Every Baptist church not only has absolute and complete freedom to prepare its own covenant but also should exercise this privilege to achieve maximum covenantal benefit. Baptist publishers can help churches more by sponsoring the concept of writing personalized covenants than by encouraging them to align themselves with uniform covenants. To sum up, a Baptist church is under no authoritative obligation to use a covenant which comes from a source outside its own membership.

At least four distinct values can come about when a church takes the initiative to write its own covenant. The first is that a church can give more emphasis and clarity to its covenant commitments and disciplines. Members can creatively portray in summary format biblical standards and principles by which they intend to guide their lives. The church which prepares its own covenant can concretize the personal commitments it considers to have highest priority and can provide the kind of clarification and stress that will make its covenant a meaningful document and a functional tool for moral and spiritual growth.

A second value of a personally written covenant is that it can reflect the unique needs and expectations of the church drawing it up. A church can create a covenant that has close kinship to the actual situation of its members and that is realistic in terms of the intentions of the members. If a covenant is constructed around the specific needs of a congregation, it will be a more viable and useful document.

It is unrealistic to think that the covenant of J. Newton Brown, which is well over 120 years old and which gives a poor treatment of social issues, can presume to meet the vastly different needs of thousands of modern Baptist churches. No covenant written by one person can adequately meet the ethical requirements of changing congregations in a fluctuating world. A church covenant must be a congregational enterprise in order to produce the best results. A church covenant is the covenant of a group, and it is corporate participation in the formation of a covenant that gives it its deepest meaning for a church. One writer was on target when he affirmed that "a covenant will have more meaning and value if its content is designed by members of the congregation. When each sentence and paragraph has been carefully weighed and discussed, a covenant will have greater significance and enduring value." [8]

A third value of writing a covenant is that this process can contribute to the moral and spiritual renewal of a congregation. There has clearly been a resurgence of interest in the church covenant concept among Baptists within the last decade, and much of this has likely been due to Baptist participation in the church renewal movement, which began its ascendency on the American religious scene in the early 1960s. A Baptist pastor in Ohio recently wrote, "My own personal convictions [about church covenants] have grown over the past decade as I have read much in the area of church renewal." [9] The covenant idea fits easily into the context of renewal. The very nature and responsible use of a covenant presuppose the motif of continuing renewal of one's pledges relating to conduct. This achievement of renewal is enhanced when a church writes its own covenant.

A fourth value which can result when a church writes its own covenant is that certain covenant practices may become stronger. This writer recently performed a limited survey to determine the uses made of church covenants by Southern Baptist churches. Of the 217 churches responding to a questionnaire, only ten used covenants which they had written. Still, these ten churches had stronger covenant practices in eight instances than the churches using uniform covenants. [10] Thirty-five percent more of the former used covenants in the Lord's Supper. Twenty-two percent more read covenants responsively or in unison in worship services. Twenty-two percent more used covenants in new member orientation classes. Fifteen percent more employed covenants in the act of admitting new members. Ten percent more had pastors who had recently delivered a sermon or given a prayer meeting talk on a covenant. Eight percent more invited new members to sign a covenant. Eight percent more disciplined members for serious violations of covenantal agreements. Last, two percent more used covenants in baptism.

A logical deduction from these findings of the survey is that the strength of many covenant practices is heavily contingent on the approach which churches take in arriving at agreeable covenants. The church which relies on the internal creativity of its membership in preparing a covenant will probably have more effective covenant practices than a church which perfunctorily adopts an outside, uniform covenant that contains pledges and promises which are not necessarily related to the particular needs of the church.

HOW TO PREPARE A CHURCH COVENANT

Baptists desperately need to restore the practice by which each church writes and adopts its own covenant. What procedures can a church follow to get this accomplished? Six steps seem appropriate for designing an acceptable covenant.

1. Create interest in writing a church covenant by demonstrating its potential values. A pastor can do this through a series of sermons on the covenant idea—exploring biblical, historical, theological, and practical ramifications of the idea. Deacons can do this by first of all writing and adopting a deacons' covenant expressing disciplines of conduct to which they, as the church's servants and spiritual leaders, are willing to align themselves. Diaconal commitment to a covenantal pattern will provide a model by which the larger congregation can establish its own disciplines. Further, a study class in a church can devote several consecutive meetings to a study of the church covenant concept. This class can be the interest center from which evolves a broader look at covenants by an entire church. Once the values of covenanting become visible, a church will be more willing to take a hard look at its own covenantal status and consider the preparation of its personal covenantal document.

2. Appoint a church covenant committee. The pastor, deacons, or a study group cannot assume the prerogative to prepare a covenant for the church. Apart from official approval by the church, any covenant would have limited authority and appeal for the greater congregation. A better approach is for the church in business session—as the result of a recommendation by the deacons or some other group—to elect a church covenant committee whose work will be to coordinate the designing and printing of a covenantal statement. This committee will be responsible to the church at every level of its functioning.

Since the new committee will work to prepare a *church* covenant, the committee should be composed of a broad spectrum of the total church membership. Representatives of both sexes and of various age levels (from youth to senior citizens) should be placed on the committee. This balance will help insure that the final covenant will have wide appeal to all church members. The essential characteristic of each member of the committee should be that the quality of his or her witness as a church member is beyond reproach. The committee will be preparing an implement that will serve to nurture integrity in church membership, and this requires that the committee possess credentials reflecting indisputable moral and spiritual character.

3. Adopt principles by which the content of the covenant will be determined. The committee will need to establish at the outset that nothing will be placed in the covenant which does not have a biblical foundation. This will guarantee that the covenant will complement, rather than replace, basic themes of the Bible relating to Christian conduct. A covenant does not create new tasks for Christians; it summarizes biblical responsibilities which are applicable to contemporary life. The committee will also need to decide whether to concentrate on positive features of Christian conduct that are to be imitated or on negative features of non-Christian conduct that are to be avoided. Covenants based on the latter thrust offer no affirmative guidance; those rooted in the former approach magnify the ethical truths of the Bible and legitimatize adherence to them.

Should a covenant be phrased mainly in terms of general or specific responsibilities? The committee has to resolve this question quickly. A covenant which is extremely specific in naming personal sins to avoid, all the social issues which need

Christian involvement, and other matters runs the risk of being too legal, long, and narrow in scope and application. A covenant which is extremely general can be so ambiguous as to be meaningless. Perhaps the following guideline can be helpful in structuring a covenant. A covenant ought to be specific enough to state concrete commitments, disciplines, and expectations, but it should be general enough to allow for flexibility in interpretation. This will state the position of the church on matters of conduct and, at the same time, give priority to the Baptist concept of the priesthood of believers.

Only those things which are basic and universal for Christian life should be included in a covenant. "Trifling things and customs based upon peculiar cultural conditions ought not to be included in its obligations." [11] A covenant can function best if its individual elements are viewed as biblical principles which guide conduct rather than as rules which govern conduct. It is a misuse of a covenant to treat it as a legal document. The strength of a covenant does not lie in a legalistic attachment to its wording but in a reliance upon the biblical principles which lie behind the wording.

4. Define and write the contents of the covenant. Make explicit at the beginning that the covenant is foremost a covenant with God and then a group of vows made to fellow church members. The prominence of the theological aspect accents the cruciality of taking the covenant seriously. Since covenants have been published in conjunction with confessions of faith throughout Baptist history, the implication is that there must be healthy interaction between doctrine and conduct. A covenant is concerned primarily with conduct, but it ideally has a strong biblical and theological foundation that is authentically Trinitarian. For this reason, a brief statement of basic Christian beliefs is entirely appropriate in a covenant. Doctrinal assertions frequently appear in the opening sections of covenants.

Ideally, the contents of a covenant are comprehensive in scope. Principles for conduct in all phases of life are displayed in a healthy covenantal agreement. In examining eleven church covenants of seventeenth-century English Baptists, this writer found four broad categories of emphasis: church fellowship, church discipline, worship and personal devotion, and pastoral and lay care. These same themes have extended themselves through the centuries and are primary to many modern covenants. A social consciousness also pervades some of the best contemporary covenants. As a minimum, covenants need to include pledges relating to our personal lives, our families, our social lives, our church, our pastoral concern for others, and primarily to our God. A sound sense of preventive discipline underlies all these vows. Each church will need to word its vows in its own unique way.

5. Secure congregational input and approval. After several meetings, a church covenant committee will draw up a preliminary draft of a covenant. This draft should use words understandable by the youngest members of the church while expressing content that will challenge even the most mature members. If this does not seem possible, the committee may wish to prepare two covenants similar in content but different in wording—one for children and the other for youth and adults. The committee will find it valuable and instructive to reproduce a copy of the preliminary draft for each member of the church. Accompanying the draft should be a brief statement of the principles upon which it is grounded. Members should be encouraged to study the draft carefully and to write down any responsible criticisms they wish to make. The committee will receive the evaluations, weigh them carefully, pen a second draft incorporating the best suggestions, distribute the second draft for further suggestions, modify the statement as needed, and then write a final draft for presentation to the church in an official business session. The final draft should be handed out to church members well in advance of the business meeting designated for its discussion. Verbal discussion in the meeting may lead to additional alterations in the contents. The vote approving the covenant will ideally be unanimous, but compromise may be required with some of its elements in order to achieve unanimity. Congregational involvement, such as that just described, in the formation of a covenant will make certain that the covenant is a *church* covenant, not a *committee* covenant.

6. Print and circulate the covenant. A handy procedure is to print the covenant on small cards. Each card should at least contain the name of the church, its location, the date of the covenant's adoption, and the covenant. Cards can be given to all members, including nonresidents, with a statement describing the development and purpose of the covenant. Other cards can be attached to the inside covers of hymnals so that they will be

available as worship aids. Some church classes may choose to have the covenant printed in large letters in the form of a wall chart for easy reference.

Even after a church writes a covenant, it should be subject to continuing modification. No church covenant has canonical status, in spite of the tendency of many Baptists to ascribe definitive authority and official standing to selected uniform covenants. The Kittery Church, formed in 1682 as the first Baptist church in Maine, registered its intention to meet the duties contained in the covenant adopted at its formation, but it also indicated a willingness to accept new obligations which God might subsequently reveal to its members.[12] A progressive principle needs to be incorporated into the making of each covenant. New illumination by the Holy Spirit, the development of new needs and areas of emphasis within a church, and the requirement of keeping the language of a covenant updated are only a few of the factors which may necessitate periodic modification of a covenant.

IMPLEMENTING CHURCH COVENANTS

Unless a church intends to implement its covenant, there is little value in preparing and adopting one. To advance covenant practices only as far as the formal exercise of reading covenants responsively or in unison on an occasional basis offers minimal help in confronting problems of integrity in church membership. "If it is a mere formality, the occasional public reading of the covenant becomes all but meaningless."[13]

A fundamental assumption is that every regenerated Christian who joins a Baptist church automatically takes on essential responsibilities to God, the church, and the world. These duties are integral to individual discipleship and to the nature and mission of the church and cannot be treated casually, postponed, or ignored. Rather, service and contributions to God, the church, and the world must have high priority in the life of each member. The accomplishing of such ministries and disciplines as regular attendance in Bible study and worship, responsible stewardship, sensitive caring, and exemplary living is foundational to the well-being of God's church and God's world. Careful covenantal implementation is one way to guarantee that these and other ministries and disciplines will become fully activated and effective.

Probably the best approach to covenantal practices and implementation is a continuing and comprehensive approach for all members. Covenantal principles which function by guiding Christian conduct need to permeate all phases of church life. Church members of all ages should sense the gravity of covenantal pledges and the need to live up to them. The covenantal thrust should be so widespread that prospective members can easily see that membership in a church means vastly more than nominal attachment to a church role. A church will do well to make no covenantal demands on new members that it is unwilling to make on veteran members. To do so both creates a double standard of ethics for members and falsifies the legitimacy of covenanting as being applicable to the total church. The "do because I told you so and don't ask any questions" philosophy will not hold water with new members. Covenant practices require full participation by all members.

Possible forms of covenantal implementation are numerous. Baptism, the Lord's Supper, church discipline, evangelism, and small groups are such important areas of covenantal cultivation that the remaining chapters of the book are devoted to these subjects. Specific covenantal practices to be explored at this point include signing covenants, using covenants in constituting new churches, developing special covenant meetings, and living out the contents of a covenant.

Real strength can be given a covenant by having every member sign it voluntarily at the time of its adoption and by having every subsequent member sign it voluntarily at the time of his or her formal admission into the church. This practice can stimulate a firmer affinity with covenantal principles and bonds on the part of all members. A few churches are even sponsoring an annual membership which hinges on a member's willingness to renew his or her covenant each year by re-signing it. Only an exceptionally mature congregation can accept this particular practice, but it can have enormously valuable results in maintaining a regenerate and disciplined membership.

The signing of covenants presently exists in only a very small percentage of Baptist churches. The failure to sign covenants may suggest a prevalent denial of covenantal validity. Also, in the popular mind, as this writer has discovered in conversations with many people, a creedal idea is often negatively associated with covenants. Considering the Baptist aversion to creeds, this association may contribute to an unwillingness both to sponsor and to write covenants. This is unfortunate, for a church covenant has absolutely no creedal connections. Since its predominant concern is conduct, it is not subject to creedal relationships. For this reason, a church can encourage members to sign its covenant without any fear of creedal impingement or violation of Baptist polity. The most likely reason that churches hesitate to sponsor the signing of covenants is that this requires placing one's name on the dotted line of spiritual and ethical demand. If members do not sign, they do not feel so rigidly tied down to basic commitments of faith and work. Thus, not signing may be the easy way out of denying self and taking up the cross.

By contrast, the precedents of Baptist history fully certify the acceptance, workability, and values of signing covenants. In early English Baptist churches, covenants tended to be signed by charter members in the process of forming new churches.[14] Frequently, persons who later united with a church also signed its covenant. Morgan Edwards, earliest historian of Baptists in America, probably described the general practices of colonial Baptists when he recommended in 1774 that charter members should sign a covenant, that a person subsequently joining a church should also sign, and that an excommunicated person should re-sign a covenant if allowed to rejoin a church.[15] The signing of covenants by early Baptists tied them quite closely to their voluntary agreements. This is a practice which can well be imitated today. It is one way of insisting that church members pay honorable attention to the ethical demands and principles of conduct that are incumbent upon them.

Another way Baptists can implement their covenants, besides signing them, is to recognize their worth in defining a church and therefore to make them key elements in constituting new churches. The church covenant idea is integral to the nature of a church and inheres in the essence of congregational life. A brief historical survey will accelerate an understanding of the accuracy of this claim among Baptists of the past. In order to see how a covenant can exercise a vital role as a constitutive element of a church's organization, one must first know the role of covenants in Baptist ecclesiology.

To begin with, confessions of faith of two important Baptist churches in America in the 1660s and the 1750s clearly linked covenanting with definitions of the church. The confession of the First Baptist Church of Boston, which was constituted in 1665, stated that the proper subjects for a church are those who have "gladly received the word" and baptism, "and a competent number of such joyned together in Covenant & fellowship of the gospel are a Church of Christ."[16] Further, the confession of the Middleborough Separate Baptist Church, formed in Massachusetts in 1756 with the famous Isaac Backus as its pastor, identified a church as a group of Christians "by mutual acquaintance & communion voluntarily and understandingly covenanting & embodying together for the carrying on [of] the Worship & Service of God."[17]

In 1774 two key writings furthered the pattern being described. Morgan Edwards said forthrightly that "a covenant is the formal cause of a church: so that without a covenant, expressed or implied, a visible church there cannot be."[18] David Thomas, a leader of the Regular Baptists in Virginia, listed five elements which he considered necessary for the being of a Baptist church: a certain number of persons, at least two or three; a profession of faith on the part of each member; proper baptism, namely, believer's baptism by immersion in the name of the Trinity; submission to the imposition of hands; and the joining together in a mutual covenant.[19]

Baptists of the nineteenth and twentieth centuries have perpetuated the identification of covenanting with the nature of the church. The New Hampshire Confession of Faith, as modified by J. Newton Brown in 1853, which became the most influential confession among Baptists in America in the latter 1800s, affirmed that a church is "a congregation of baptized believers, associated by covenant in the faith and fellowship of the Gospel. . . ."[20] This same emphasis continued in the doctrinal statements adopted by the Southern Baptist Convention in 1925 and 1963.[21]

The point is obvious. Baptist churches have a covenantal foundation. If this foundation is lacking, a church has either lost or abandoned an essential part of its identity. Knowing that by definition a Baptist church has a covenantal substructure which insures that members have duties to God and one another is reason enough to incorporate a covenantal document, along with a confession of faith, charter, constitution, bylaws, and other documents, into the actual process of constituting a church. When a congregation views a covenant as integral to its origin and self-understanding, then the church has a useful document for assuring integrity in its membership.

How can a group of Baptists be convinced of the need to make a covenant a meaningful part of the formation of a new church? For one thing, they need to realize that a church comes into being in stages and that a covenant has a proper place in these stages. Maring and Hudson have quite helpfully labeled three stages comprising the constitutive development of a church. First, Baptists become a church *"essential"* when they formally express in a covenant their intention to be a church. Second, they become a church *"completed"* after adopting a constitution and electing officers. Third, they become a church *"recognized"* after admission into a Baptist association.[22] The reader sees quickly that a church covenant is critical to the first stage of organizing a new church. No subsequent stage makes sense unless this step reaches culmination.

Further encouragement for using covenants in forming new churches can come by studying the literature of Baptist history and seeing numerous examples of this being done. Morgan Edwards and David Thomas described in 1774 in separate writings model ways to constitute a church. Both believed that the day for forming a church should be set aside by fasting. The service of constitution should then include the presence of an assisting minister, prayer, a probing into the qualifications of the candidates for membership and questions about their intentions to live disciplined lives, joint participation in a covenant, the signing of the covenant, and a pronouncement by the officiating minister that the covenanters were officially a church.[23]

A live illustration of a new church making a covenant the heart of its constitutive procedure appears in the earliest records of the First Baptist Church of Warren, Rhode Island. Constituted on November 14, 1764, on a day set aside for fasting, the service of organization involved prayers; a sermon; and the presentation, reading, and signing of a covenant. The assisting minister, James Manning, who became the first pastor of the church, then asked the persons who had signed the covenant whether they received it as their "plan of union in a church relation, which question was answered by them all in the affirmative, standing up."[24]

Evidence is indisputable that the acceptance of covenantal vows has been basic to the establishing of Baptist churches in America. The practice must continue and be taken seriously if new churches are to possess a biblical type of solidarity around guidelines for Christian conduct. After sharing in the adoption of a covenant in organizing the Middleborough Baptist church in Massachusetts on January 16, 1756, Isaac Backus wrote that "my soul had a very weighty sense of the greatness of the affairs before us and of the infinite importance of carefully keeping to the rules of Christ's house both in admitting members, and also in after dealings with them."[25] Modern Baptists will do well to capture the sensitive concern of Backus that initial covenantal agreements will continue indefinitely. A church covenant is not a document whose value comes from being used once in the formation of a church and then being placed in a cornerstone only to be discovered by a later generation of members. Rather, a covenant is a living agreement whose biblical principles offer permanent sustenance for a church genuinely trying to be regenerate. Baptist history validates this possibility.

A third way to implement a covenant, besides signing it or using it in a church's formation, is to make it the focal point of special covenant meetings. Baptist churches in some sections of the country used to hold covenant meetings on a weekday prior to the Sunday in which the churches held their monthly observance of the Lord's Supper. The meetings had at least four purposes. They prepared church members for participation in the Lord's Supper on the following Sunday. They reminded members of covenantal obligations. They gave members a chance to share meaningful spiritual experiences of the previous month. And they provided members with a monthly opportunity to renew and strengthen covenantal pledges. "The recovery of such a practice today could help to impress upon us the significance of our covenant obligations and prepare us for a more meaningful celebration of the Lord's Supper."[26]

The neglect of covenant meetings today is probably, in part, a result of the multiplication of other church meetings. Prayer meetings, business meetings, and committee meetings, for example, occupy much of the time formerly given to covenantal emphases. This need not be the case, however. In preparation for the Lord's Supper, the prayer meeting on the Wednesday night (or other night) preceding this event could easily be reconverted into the covenant meeting it once was among Baptists in many places. In the covenant meeting, a church could read, study, and explore its covenant and grasp its implications for sharing in the Lord's Supper and in daily living.

Several suggestions may be helpful for developing a covenant meeting. The first five are adapted from Augustine Carman's *The Covenant and the Covenant Meeting;*[27] the second five are original with the present writer. The purpose of the suggestions is to make a covenant meeting as effective as possible. (1) The meeting should be different from a prayer meeting where only a few participate. Everyone should be encouraged to participate, but no one should be forced to do so. (2) The meeting should be understood to be a family or fellowship meeting of the church. (3) It should be a time for introspection and the sharing of personal experiences, both positive and negative. (4) The entire covenant should be read at each meeting. (5) Various clauses and themes in the covenant can receive special attention in successive meetings. (6) Study of the biblical background of elements in the covenant should also be prominent. (7) The covenantal thrust and values of the Lord's Supper ought to be explored in detail. (8) Ways of strengthening the regenerate character of church membership should be hammered out on a continuing basis. (9) Reaffirmation of the covenantal qualities of congregational life should occur through making regular commitments to God and one another. (10) Direction for activating the contents of the covenant in daily living should be sought through extensive sessions of prayer.

Various efforts have been made to show the importance of covenant meetings. Carman cited a biblical verse which he believed gave support to such meetings, especially as preparation for the Lord's Supper, "Let a man examine himself, and so eat of the bread and drink of the cup" (1 Corinthians 11:28). He then described the covenant meeting as "the heart of the devotional life of a Baptist church."[28] Edward T. Hiscox, the famous writer of Baptist church manuals in the latter 1800s, concurred with Carman's assessment of covenant meetings. Hiscox stated that if a member could attend only two church services in a month, he should give first priority to the Lord's Supper and second to the covenant meeting.[29] Perhaps the evaluations of these men coupled with the suggestions given in the preceding paragraphs can create a new interest in covenant meetings among Baptists.

A fourth, and probably the most important, way to implement a church covenant is to live out its contents in daily experiences. It is of little consequence for a covenant to be signed, to be used in the formation of a church, or to be studied in covenant meetings if a congregation does not intend to make the biblical principles of its covenant fully operative in its total life. The seriousness of the obligations assumed in becoming a member of a church which has Jesus Christ as Lord demands covenantal embodiment and fulfillment in the affairs of life. Proper approach to a covenant magnifies the ethics of church membership and engineers spiritual maturation. The point made by a writer in referring to the early Baptists in New Jersey has equal validity for Baptists today: "While church members were not expected to be perfect, they were expected to do their best to be faithful to their covenant obligations."[30] A covenant worth having is a covenant worth living.

The Swansea Baptist Church formed in Rehoboth, Massachusetts, as the fourth Baptist church in America, adopted at its organization in 1663 a covenant which is the earliest extant covenant among Baptists in America. In the heart of this covenant is a comprehensive pledge which contemporary Baptists will do well to imitate in deciding what status to give their covenantal promises. The covenant reads, "We will henceforth endeavor to perform all our respective duties towards God and each other. . . ."[31] The implication is obvious that a church which takes a responsible approach to its covenant will try extremely hard to meet in daily life the demands of Christian discipleship delineated in the covenant.

If a covenant calls for (1) firm attachment to the doctrines and ordinances of a church; (2) regular attendance at church worship; (3) faithful contributions of time, talents, and money; (4) committed involvement in the ministries of the church; (5) personal attention to living Christlike lives, meeting God daily in prayer and Bible study, and treating our bodies as the temple of the Holy Spirit; (6) the creation and nurture of a Christian atmosphere in our homes; (7) the exertion of Christian influence upon the life of our communities; (8) bearing a deliberate witness to non-Christians; or (9) any one of a whole host of other important moral and spiritual challenges, then covenanters with integrity will apply their fundamental energies to accomplishing these very objectives. The quality of church membership will surely improve once there is a proper linkup between a statement of ethical intentions and lives of achievement.

A recurring theme in the New Testament is a call for the people of God to cultivate consistency between the truth they hear and proclaim and the actions they perform. Jesus concluded the Sermon on the Mount with the story of a wise man who built a house on a rock and a foolish man who constructed his on the sand. Wisdom in this parable equaled hearing and doing God's word. Foolishness was hearing and not doing God's word. James later echoed this motif in calling for hearers of the word to be doers and in labeling as self-deception the act of hearing and not doing. To write, adopt, and read a biblically based church covenant without doing the truth expressed in it is congregational folly. To actualize the contents of this same covenant in concrete living is pure exemplification of congregational wisdom.

Miscellaneous other ways to implement a church covenant are also appropriate. Church training classes can study a covenant. A pastor can occasionally deliver a sermon on the church's covenant. A church can periodically read its covenant in worship services. A church can even designate a certain Sunday during the year to be the annual church covenant day. The largest Baptist church in the Southern Baptist Convention, the First Baptist Church of Dallas, Texas, has such a day. The "Church Covenant Day" occurs on the Sunday before the spring revival when the church celebrates the Lord's Supper. The members read the covenant together and publicly renew their pledges to its faithful observance. "It is a day of recommitment on the part of the entire membership." [32]

3

Church Membership in Celebration

Believer's baptism and the Lord's Supper are essential to planting and growing integrity in church life. The common theology behind both ordinances is that active faith in Jesus Christ must precede participation in the ordinances. Baptism is, in effect, a covenant with God and the church. The Lord's Supper is reaffirmation and extension of that covenant. Those who receive the ordinances voluntarily oblige themselves to certain Christian commitments and standards. The church, in turn, assumes obligations to the participants. The heart and vitality of a regenerate church membership hinge heavily on the intensity with which Christians remain true to their baptismal and Lord's Supper vows, and on the degree to which churches insist that their ,nembers adhere to these vows.

Responsible use of baptism and the Lord's Supper enables Christian confession, obedience, and fellowship to become a reality. Overreaction to the application of a sacramental value to the ordinances by some religious bodies sometimes causes Baptists to treat the ordinances irresponsibly. This occurs by reducing their doctrinal foundation to mere symbol, by providing insufficient advance training in the requirements of church membership for participants, by minimizing the practical importance of the ordinances for creating and sustaining invigorated Christians and churches, by administering the ordinances far too casually, and by allowing extremely young children (including three-year-olds) to share in them.

The trend toward allowing younger and younger children in Baptist life to share in the ordinances is a particularly devastating menace to the basic Baptist principle that the ordinances are reserved for believers. Toddlers are incapable of making responsible decisions about matters of ultimate spiritual significance. Further, their spiritual innocence precludes the need for them to make such decisions. Only those persons accountable for their spiritual condition, repentant of personal sin, responsive to God's forgiveness, and eager to find fulfillment through faith in God, Christian commitment, and allegiance to the church can experience the true meaning of the ordinances. To allow premature participation of very young children in the ordinances is an open invitation for many of these children to grow up with little understanding of even the fundamental claims of the ordinances upon their life-styles. Further, the allowance of such premature participation is a sad commentary on the regenerate status of many congregations.

What relationship do believer's baptism and the Lord's Supper have with a regenerate church membership? They help guarantee its preservation when viewed and used properly. Apart from scrupulous implementation of these ordinances, the church can easily become filled with the nonregenerate. If this happens, the church undercuts its high standards for membership, and the nonregenerate receive the privileges and duties of the household of faith without possessing adequate credentials for doing so. The painful result is that the church moves further and further away from the New Testament model. We can observe the unhappy results of this process in some contemporary Baptist churches.

Believer's baptism and the Lord's Supper are vehicles of celebration for encouraging increased attachment to Jesus Christ, his accomplishments of love for us, and the mission to which he calls us. The fidelity of Baptists to the full content of the ordinances has immediate and urgent ramifications for the quality and regenerate characteristics of Baptist life. This chapter is designed to elevate the ordinances a little closer to the important level assigned them by Jesus Christ and New Testament writers, to demonstrate their value in countering the nonregenerate ailments afflicting some Baptist churches, and to offer practical suggestions which can bring new life and meaning to them.

THE CELEBRATION OF BELIEVER'S BAPTISM

The New Testament is amply clear in showing that only believers in Christ as Lord can be proper subjects of baptism. The apostle Paul wrote to the Colossian Christians that "you were buried with him [Christ] in baptism, in which you were also raised with him through faith in the working of God . . ." (Colossians 2:12). Shortly afterwards, Paul asked the same Christians, "Why do you live as if you still belonged to the world?" (Colossians 2:20). Several factors could have led the Colossians away from their initial assertions of dedication to Christ. Is it possible that they were not adequately prepared in advance for the implications of believer's baptism for the way they should conduct themselves morally and spiritually? Perhaps not. Whatever the case, the Colossians certainly missed the long-range covenantal significance of the baptismal event. Since the current nonresident and inactive resident membership problems of Baptists suggest that the Colossian dilemma may have extended itself into a Baptist dilemma, where can we go for help?

Pre-Baptismal Instruction

A preliminary examination of those who request baptism is vitally important.[1] Candidates for church membership need to know the supreme seriousness of the venture they wish to take, and the church needs to know the motives and intentions of the candidates. Persons with weak motives and intentions can perhaps be guided toward sounder reasons for their decision. The pastor, deacons, or a church membership committee, or a combination of these, can function well in making the examination. The goal is not to weed out undesirables, but to present to all candidates the grace of God and the need for integrity in the pilgrimage they are about to make. This approach requires at the earliest stage of application for membership that candidates for baptism are truly regenerate and zealous to activate their faith in concrete ways.

A lengthy period of pre-baptismal instruction can then follow the preliminary examination. Such instruction is a healthy way to introduce baptismal candidates to the wider dimensions and expectations of the Christian life. Biblical precedent for pre-baptismal training lies in Luke's account of the encounter between Philip and the Ethiopian eunuch (Acts 8:26-40). Philip prepared the eunuch for the latter's baptism. Four features characterized this instructional happening. First, the eunuch had a preliminary responsiveness to the things of Scripture as reflected in his reading from the prophet Isaiah while riding a chariot. Second, the Spirit of God challenged Philip, who had just completed a preaching mission in Samaria, to join the eunuch in his journey. Third, Philip accepted the challenge of the Spirit, interpreted a part of Isaiah 53 to the eunuch, and used the passage as a launching pad for telling the eunuch "the good news of Jesus" (Acts 8:35). Fourth, Philip baptized the eunuch after the latter affirmed (according to some manuscripts),."I believe that Jesus Christ is the Son of God" (Acts 8:37, KJV).

The education received by the eunuch prior to his baptism was as important as the baptism itself. Without the special training from a student of Scripture and an avid practitioner of the Christian faith, the eunuch would have received an empty baptism. Fortunately, this did not occur. The Spirit of God sent a Christian into the life of the eunuch in a teachable moment. Philip taught the eunuch basic information about Jesus and the long-term meaning Jesus could have for his life. The eunuch listened eagerly and declared his faith in the Son of God. *Then came baptism!* Pre-baptismal training was foundational to Philip's approach to the eunuch. This approach can be a workable model for Baptist churches today as they confront nonregenerate membership problems arising partly from treating baptism too lightly.

Church members have vast covenantal obligations. Of primary importance is the need for prospective members to know the nature and binding quality of these obligations before baptism. To baptize and then teach church membership duties is similar to taking a college entrance examination and then studying for it. Priorities are reversed. A college entrance examination makes sense when preceded by years of careful academic preparation in high school. Baptism is entrance into the church. Instructional preparation is imperative for this experience. Without basic training for candidates, baptism can be a breeding ground for inactive church members. And frankly, "There is no more justification for having inactive members in a church than for having inactive soldiers in an army." [2]

In order for baptismal candidates to begin a responsible journey into church membership, they need to know before baptism the duties they will have. A genuine study of the commitments and disciplines which a church expects of its members should precede both the vote of a church in receiving a new member and the candidate's baptism. The voluntary element of aligning oneself with an authentic covenantal community will assume a deeper meaning for the candidate after such a study. Careless admission standards have resulted in far too many Christians being both nominal and unknowledgeable church members, and churches must assume a large portion of the blame for this predicament. Pre-baptismal training insures that candidates know what the church expects of them. Therefore, churches will do well to consider the formation of pre-baptismal classes. Several suggestions for helping such classes work will now be offered.

1. Attendance in pre-baptismal classes should be required of all persons desiring baptism. The mandatory element is essential both to add substance to membership standards and to assure each candidate that he or she is about to enter a serious covenant which must be conditioned by certain types of knowledge and commitments. This approach will help phase out the careless acceptance of members into churches. Also, candidates for membership will appreciate the classes as media through which they can share their experiences of regeneration and explore ways to live out their salvation.

A prerequisite to establishing a pre-baptismal class is to encourage present church members, regardless of age, to submit themselves to the contents of the instructional course. It cannot be supposed that all present members are fully knowledgeable on all the matters to be discussed in the class. Participation in the course by a broad spectrum of members will tighten the corporate integrity of the church. When present members have taken the course, the entire membership will have profited and the church will be on more solid ground for insisting that all subsequent candidates for membership follow suit.

The pre-baptismal study recommended here can be successful only in a mature church that is willing to abandon a casual approach to membership in favor of congregational life that is authentic, regenerated, and biblical. Church membership might not grow as rapidly once such an approach becomes operative. The real question, however, is whether it is more important for the church to fill its ranks with numerous inactive and nonresident members or to demand that all members be "the salt of the earth" and "the light of the world." In view of the need to accent regenerate features of church membership, the latter option makes more sense. The goal of the approach under consideration is not to purge church rolls of inactive members but rather to activate the spiritual potential of these people and to preclude the possibility of new members falling into the fold of the inactive.

2. Although it is not necessary for pre-baptismal instruction to last three years, as was sometimes the case in the early post-New Testament church,[3] it should cover several one-hour sessions, perhaps up to ten and possibly more. Devoting more time to examining subjects which are of vital importance to baptismal candidates will increase the possibility that they will become church members who are both informed and committed.

A church will find it valuable to hold a pre-baptismal course several times each year, depending, of course, upon the number of people presenting themselves for baptism. In this way there will never be a lag between the time a person registers the desire to be baptized and the time of enrollment in a class. The teacher of the class can be the pastor, a trained deacon, or any other member whose spiritual credentials are beyond question. Perhaps the best route is for a combination of these leaders to function in a team-teaching approach.

A second class can run simultaneously with the pre-baptismal class, while existing for a different group of people. This class is for candidates for church membership who have already been baptized by immersion, such as those transferring their allegiance from another Baptist church. This class would cover many of the same subjects included in a pre-baptismal class but would concentrate more heavily on post-baptismal Christian commitments than on the meaning of baptism itself. A church cannot afford to assume that a Baptist moving his or her membership from another church has a full understanding of the implications of a regenerate church membership. Every Baptist must be aware of the expectations the church has for him or her.

3. The subjects taught in a pre-baptismal class should be comprehensive in scope. Only a brief amount of time will be allotted to the study of each subject, but candidates for baptism will profit immeasurably by being exposed to a wide variety of subjects relating to Christian discipleship and church membership. A pre-baptismal class could easily offer selected mini-studies in the biblical, historical, theological, and practical areas, just as is done on a larger scale in the curriculum of a school of theology in a Baptist seminary. Biblical studies can focus on the meaning and demands of baptism and of being a Christian. Historical studies can center on the history of Baptists and the history of the local church into which entrance is being sought. Theological studies can pay attention to Baptist doctrine and particularly to the individual confession of faith of the church. Practical studies can concentrate on Christian ethics, opportunities for witness and ministry, and the relation of the church's covenant to Christian conduct.

Obviously, a church cannot expect a candidate for baptism to master the previously mentioned subjects in great detail; refinement in these areas of knowledge and action can come later through regular training classes offered to church members. A church does owe the candidate for baptism the right and duty to possess basic and accurate information about his or her new role as a church member. In the process of delineating membership responsibilities to applicants, a church does a noble service to the applicants by telling them they are undertaking an enterprise of ultimate consequence and to itself by firming up its qualifications for admission.

Additionally, since a pre-baptismal class will possibly be the first major exposure which membership candidates will have to the quality of teaching offered by the church, the instruction in the class should represent intelligent, thorough, and prayerful preparation which culminates in a simple and intimate presentation. Information shared ought to be palatable to the most mentally brilliant participant and easily understandable by the most immature. If a church frequently has many candidates, it may be good to have two or more classes for various age groups. At any rate, this introductory course into the life of the church should not be a slipshod and haphazard effort, but rather a spiritually thrilling and stimulating adventure for teacher and pupils alike.

Each applicant for membership deserves the best instruction and guidance the church is capable of assembling. Baptism will be far more meaningful once the course is completed.

Baptismal Pledges

Church covenants deserve more attention in the context of baptism, for baptism as an initiation into the church consists of vows to God and the church. For too long many Baptists have interpreted baptism as being merely symbolic in character. The New Testament and church history suggest that this view of baptism neglects an indispensable feature of the event, namely, that baptism is a positive act of commitment to God and the church. More than a symbol, baptism is an actualization of a Christian's intention to live out the moral and spiritual agreements inherent in regeneration. Before presenting suggestions for combining church covenants and baptism in modern life, the urgency of renewing a responsible relationship between the two demands a brief look at biblical and historical precedents which demonstrate the viability of such a union.

New Testament baptism may have had as one of its primary elements a covenant that the participant made with the Christian community and with Christ. In the baptismal initiation into church privileges and duties, the one being baptized vowed to "walk in newness of life" (Romans 6:4) and to "put on Christ" (Galatians 3:27). The baptism of Jesus gave to water baptism the new meaning of "a personal commitment to the will of God."[4]

The theology of baptism in the age of the Church Fathers centered on the person's sharing in Christ's victory over Satan and his demonic hosts through the assistance of the Holy Spirit. "*From man's side,* it [baptism] entails a vow, the meaning of the early Latin word *sacramentum.*"[5] John Chrysostom, Greek church leader of the late fourth century, repeatedly referred to baptism as a contract. Concerning the verbal rejection during baptism of the devil's domination and the acknowledgment of Christ's sovereignty by the one being baptized, Chrysostom wrote, "This was the signature, this the agreement, this the contract."[6]

Boniface, a Christian missionary to Germany in the eighth century, cautioned his hearers during a sermon to remember the promises they had made to God in baptism. He claimed that they had pledged to do such things as "believe in God," "love the

Lord," "observe the Lord's Day," "give alms," "visit the sick," "give tithes to the Church," and "receive the Eucharist."[7]

For the Continental Anabaptists of the sixteenth century, who comprised the radical wing of the Protestant Reformation, the church covenant undertaken at baptism was a pledge to obey Christ completely and was considered the supreme form of religious voluntarism other than martyrdom.[8] In 1527 Balthasar Hubmaier, one of the most influential of the Anabaptists, prepared a baptismal liturgy. As part of the liturgy, the baptismal candidate was to respond, "I will," after each of three questions asked him or her by the administrator concerning renunciation of the devil, imitation of Christ in life and conversation, and the willingness to submit to church discipline, if ever needed. Responses to these questions constituted a covenant on the part of the candidate. This covenanting immediately preceded the baptism itself.[9]

Early Baptist writings also made much reference to baptismal covenants. John Smyth, leader of the first General Baptist congregation, formed in Amsterdam about 1609, wrote in that year that "the true forme of the Church is a covenant betwixt God & the Faithful made in baptisme" and that "the covenant is this: I wilbe their Father . . . & wee shalbe his sonnes calling him Father by the Spirit, whereby we are sealed. . . ."[10] In 1675 Henry D'Anvers, an English Particular Baptist, stated that "Baptism is no other, than our Mystical *Marriage* . . . and *striking* of a Covenant (the Essentials of Marriage) betwixt Christ and a believer. . . ."[11] John Taylor, a frontier Baptist in America, witnessed in about 1770 the baptizing of over fifty people by Samuell Harriss, a Separate Baptist, at Harper's Ferry, Virginia, at which time a church covenant was read.[12]

Historical precedents for viewing baptism as a covenant which can strengthen the regenerate nature of church membership are plentiful and clear. The "so what" question is now in order. Three lessons emerging from the history of baptism and covenanting are applicable for modern Baptists.

1. Initiation into the Christian life and into church membership will be more meaningful to participants if pastors will give more adequate stress to the covenantal values of baptism. This can be done in pre-baptismal classes, in sermons, and in baptism. The theme of baptism as a beautiful picture and symbol of the death, burial, and resurrection of Christ is familiar to Baptists and is of

inestimable importance. However, baptism is more than a passive representation of events in the life of Christ; it is an active engagement of personal commitment to the claims of Christ and the church. In baptism mutual agreements among God, the church, and the one being baptized solidify themselves into a workable covenantal bond. Entrance into the church is complete only when the assumption of baptismal vows is taken most earnestly.

The results of emphasizing the covenantal values of baptism can be many. This stress can add substance to a significant, though neglected, theme of the baptismal experience. It can inform candidates from church membership that baptism requires discipleship and a strong attachment to biblical ethics. It can help Baptists move beyond the interpretation of baptism as a mere symbol. It can enhance the likelihood that a regenerate church membership will be achieved.

2. The person being baptized will find it spiritually beneficial to verbalize his or her allegiance to the contents of the church's covenant immediately prior to immersion. Rather than go through the baptismal process without saying a single word, as is frequently the case, the one being baptized is placed in a position where he or she must openly declare his or her intention before God, the church, and the administrator to meet the expectations of Christian conduct laid upon him or her by the Bible and summarized in the mutually agreed upon covenant of the church. By responding affirmatively to covenantal questions addressed just before one's actual immersion, the one being baptized shares actively and fully in the experience of church initiation. Instead of simply having something done by the administrator, one does something for God and the church by stating one's desire to coexist with both on a responsible basis. Each baptismal participant deserves the privilege to share testimony of his or her faith and to express his or her covenantal vows. This will strengthen his or her faith and cement his or her personal bond to God and the church.

3. Congregational participation needs to be maximized in the baptismal event. The usual approach in Baptist congregations is for church members to sit back in their pews and "spectate" during services of baptism. To help church members advance beyond the level of mere observation and passivity, baptismal administrators may find it advantageous to encourage them to stand together and

verbalize *continuing* covenantal responses in the way that the ones being baptized are verbalizing *initial* covenantal responses.

By definition a church covenant is a three-way bond. Just as it is important for a congregation to hear those being baptized state their intentions to identify with the patterns of Christian conduct and practice which are considered crucial to the church, it is equally important for those being baptized to hear the congregation state its intention to accept them and support them in their efforts to measure up to the biblical ideals which underlie the church's covenant. After each one being baptized has spoken to the congregation and the congregation has responded to the one being baptized, both directed by the covenantal questions of the baptismal administrator, then the administrator can complete the covenantal triangle by having the one being baptized and the congregation share their moral and spiritual pledges to God through prayer.

Baptism As Worship

The worship dimension of baptism merits special consideration. To treat baptism simply as an appendage to real worship is a critical and frequent error in some Baptist churches. To make baptism the focal point of a genuine worship experience elevates the ordinance to its proper biblical perspective. Since baptism is a worship event, every conceivable effort must be made to let God, baptismal participants, and congregational supporters interact as creatively as possible. The need to make baptismal worship as innovative and spiritually exciting as possible lies at the center of the following claims:

> A person's baptism can be the most meaningful event in his life. From that single event may come his choice of a vocation, the kind of home he builds, and the objectives toward which he directs his finest energies. Baptism signifies entry into the Christian life with all the privileges and responsibilities thereunto appertaining.[13]

Baptists have different views on the meaning of baptism. Virtually all Baptists insist that Christ himself provided the authority for baptism (Matthew 28:19), that baptism is for believers only (Acts 2:38-39), and that there is symbolic value in baptism (as evidenced in the mode of immersion). Baptism has other meanings also. One Baptist theologian traced the baptismal theme through the New Testament and found relationships of baptism to motifs such as purification (Acts 22:16), incorporation into the body of Christ (1 Corinthians 12:12-13), illumination (Hebrews 6:4), regeneration (Titus 3:5), and salvation (1 Peter 3:21).[14] In each of these instances the primacy of faith prior to baptism is assumed.

A crucial work of Baptist pastors is to translate the various meanings of baptism into major celebrations of worship. The supreme goal of baptismal worship is to create an environment in which those being baptized can participate fully in the victory of Christ over Satan and the demonic through the gift of the Holy Spirit. Baptismal worship should be an absolutely thrilling and unforgettable experience in the life of every Christian.

How does one relate the theology of baptism to the practice of baptism? The possibilities are limitless, and each pastor needs to think through the matter personally. An illustration, however, of what can be done grows out of the relationship between baptism and salvation as depicted in 1 Peter 3:21: "Baptism . . . now saves you, not as a removal of dirt from the body but as an appeal to God for a clear conscience, through the resurrection of Jesus Christ." The verse states clearly that the ceremonial washing of baptism does not save. The controlling principle of baptism is "an appeal to God for a clear conscience, through the resurrection of Jesus Christ." The English Revised Version translates the Greek word *eperōtēma* as "interrogation," rather than "appeal." "The interrogation . . . possibly reflects the practice of confessing one's faith as a part of the baptismal rite."[15] Thus, the saving act of Christ's death and resurrection coupled with a confession of faith in baptism reveal how salvation and baptism are related.

One way to translate this idea into practice is to incorporate into a baptismal service direct questions to candidates about their faith, as well as statements of faith by the candidates. This can be done either in the baptismal pool or in an engaging dialogue between baptismal candidates and the pastor and deacons in the part of the worship service preceding the ordinance. Questions and answers about the integrity of candidates' faith before the congregation will add increased significance to the whole thrust of baptism. A time for each candidate to give a brief testimony of his or her faith will enhance the value of baptism for the person. Acknowledgment of the paramount importance of God and the church by the candidates will insure that baptism is worship.

Let us take another baptismal meaning—illumination (Mark

1:10). Why not concretize this abstract idea into visible practice by careful lighting effects during baptismal worship? The lights in the building can be dimmed as each candidate is immersed. As the candidate is raised from the water, the lights can be turned on brightly. After the baptizing of all the candidates, the choir can sing a stirring rendition of "The Light of the World Is Jesus." This special use of lights and music can add an attractive dimension to baptismal worship.

Since baptism is worship, key elements which make Christian worship should be present—reading of Scriptures, comments on their meanings, prayers, hymns, and congregational participation. Added features can be a questioning of the candidates, their responses, and a verbal covenantal pact between the ones being baptized and the congregation. (See Appendix C for a suggested order of service for baptismal worship which includes all the preceding elements.) The focal point of baptismal worship is the ordinance itself. In the setting of worship, immersion can truly be a "door" into the Christian life and church membership. Candidates should not be hastened through the door, nor should they be allowed to sneak through it. Rather, they should march through it with dignity as God and fellow worshipers share in this victorious assertion of Christian commitment.

THE CELEBRATION OF THE LORD'S SUPPER

"It is not uncommon for Baptists to read a church covenant today in connection with their observance of the Lord's Supper, but this usage is often little more than a formality." [16] Assuming the accuracy of this indictment, what steps can contemporary Baptists take to revitalize the covenantal thrust of the Lord's Supper? Further, what is the relationship of this thrust to maintaining a regenerate church membership?

The Lord's Supper and Covenanting

First, one must recognize that the covenantal motif is integral to the New Testament approach to the Lord's Supper. The accounts of the Supper in Luke 22:20 and 1 Corinthians 11:25 refer to the cup as the "new covenant" in the blood of Christ. These accounts are based upon the covenantal theology of the prophets (Jeremiah 31:33f.). The new covenant was to be written on the hearts of men, rather than on stones, and was to issue in sacrifice.

"The Lord's Supper affirms a covenant in which the Lord and his disciples . . . give themselves in loving sacrifice."[17]

The Mark-Matthew account of the Lord's Supper (Mark 14:24; Matthew 26:28) has the covenantal theology of the Torah as its basis.[18] Just as the use of sacrificial blood served to ratify the mutual pledges of the old covenant (Exodus 24:8), and just as a joint meal served to complete this ratification (Exodus 24:11), the sacrificial motif in the Lord's Supper is related to the establishing and confirming of relationships in the new covenant. God covenants through Christ, and the believer reciprocates.[19] "The Lord's Supper is, before all, a symbol of communion, a brotherly covenant among table companions."[20]

Second, one must acknowledge the perpetuation in church history of the covenantal theme in Lord's Supper practices. Illustrations from two eras of this history will suffice. In the age of the Church Fathers, just as baptism was considered the means of creating a covenantal vow with the Christian community, the Lord's Supper was the means of renewing the vow. Immediately after being baptized, a new Christian shared in his first Lord's Supper, including the receiving of milk and honey.[21] This symbolized personal identification with the covenant of God. The covenantal character of the Lord's Supper resulted in the adoption of obligations. A church manual of the fourth century admonished: "Let those who take the Offering [Lord's Supper] be exhorted . . . to be careful to do good works, to love strangers, to labour in fasting, and in every good work to engage in servitude."[22]

In 1527 the Anabaptist leader Balthasar Hubmaier wrote "A Formula for the Lord's Supper." This liturgy contained ten sections, the eighth of which was a love vow, or covenant.[23] The covenant consisted of practical questions dealing with obligations and conduct to which the participants responded, "I will." This covenanting came just before the blessing and sharing of the bread and cup. Besides being a grateful remembrance of the deeds of Christ in behalf of mankind, the Lord's Supper was also for Hubmaier "a love feast through which one pledges his willingness to serve Christ in works of compassion and mercy to other men."[24]

In addition to general church history, Baptist history is also saturated with examples of churches using covenants in the setting of the Lord's Supper. Church covenant meetings, which flourished among Baptists in the 1800s, were intended to prepare church members for participation in the Lord's Supper. More recently, in a survey which I performed on church covenants, I discovered that of 217 responding Southern Baptist pastors 43 percent said "yes" when asked, "Do you ever read or mention your covenant in the setting of the Lord's Supper?"[25]

Third, practical action designed to incorporate meaningful covenanting into the Lord's Supper must occur. Two suggestions may help. To begin with, a pastor can educate the congregation in pre-baptismal classes, sermons, and Lord's Supper observances on the covenantal character of the ordinance and on the content of the church's covenant. Next, if a church celebrates the Lord's Supper in the same worship service in which it baptizes new members, then the covenantal themes of the two ordinances can be merged into a united thrust. After the baptismal participants and the congregation verbalize mutual vows in the baptismal setting (see Appendix C), the Lord's Supper can include a presentation of framed copies of the church's covenant to each person who has just been baptized. If a church celebrates baptism and the Lord's Supper in separate worship services, the Supper can still include a presentation of framed covenants to members receiving the bread and cup for the first time. The pastor can then give a covenantal charge to the entire congregation which can include a reading of the church covenant, either in unison or responsively. This will provide to all members a regular reminder of the pledges comprising the covenant. The church may also wish to present to each person sharing in the Lord's Supper for the first time the Communion cup from which he or she drank. Displayed in a prominent spot in the new member's home, the cup can be a steady reminder of the vows undertaken on this holy occasion.

The preservation of a regenerate church membership will be assisted strongly by a continuing covenantal emphasis in Lord's Supper experiences. Functioning as a composite of Christian commitments, a church covenant uniformly acknowledged and absorbed in the context of the Lord's Supper can convert the Supper from an ordinance which may seem an empty discipline to some worshipers into an act of consecration. Covenantal challenges accepted with grace can help to circumvent and preclude the problems of inactive and nonresident members. This is sufficient reason for taking the covenantal aspect of the Lord's Supper less routinely and more in earnest.

A Baptist scholar has demonstrated through an examination of the New Testament that the Lord's Supper has a past significance in its summons to covenant and recollection, a present significance in its call to thanksgiving and participation, and a future significance in its appeal to the kingdom of God and the coming of Christ. He continued, "The Lord's Supper [is] a covenant meal in which the Lordship of Christ and our commitment to do his will are brought again and again to the worshiping congregation."[26] In a sense the covenant idea is foundational to all the other meanings of the Lord's Supper.

Deacons and the Lord's Supper

Deacons are in a unique position to give to the Lord's Supper a degree of worth which it may not have in some churches. Common weaknesses in approaching the Lord's Supper include: (1) inadequate spiritual preparation by the congregation, (2) observing the meal regularly at a time other than on Sunday morning when a higher percentage of members are present, (3) rushing through the event too quickly, (4) inadequate attention to the major biblical themes surrounding the meal, (5) a feeling by the congregation that they are spectators having something done to them rather than participants reaffirming their faith in God, and (6) a lack of intense spiritual reflection (focusing on confession of sin, pleas for forgiveness, renewal of commitments, and thanksgiving for God's act of love through Christ) by church members. Deacons can combat these weaknesses and help make the Lord's Supper a cherished point of worship. A truly regenerate church membership prepares itself spiritually for the Supper, engages in creative and honest dialogue with God during the meal, and invests itself in multiple ministries of compassion as a result of the "love strength" gained in the Supper. The cultivation of a regenerate approach to the Lord's Supper can be one of the finest gifts deacons can present to a congregation.

Most Baptists are familiar with the role of deacons in distributing the bread and the cup to the congregation. In some churches whose worship services are either on radio or television, deacons even distribute the Supper to homebound members who are listening to or watching the worship service of their church. The work of deacons in assisting with the Lord's Supper has precedents from the beginnings of Baptist life in America. The

Pennepack Church was formed in 1688 in Pennsylvania as the mother Baptist church of the Middle Colonies. The usual custom in this church was for the deacons to provide bread and wine for the Lord's Supper from money collected at the previous celebration of the meal. During the Supper the deacons received the elements from the pastor and distributed them to the congregation.[27] The role of deacons in the Lord's Supper was placed in the larger context of diaconal duties in an ordination prayer for three deacons in the First Baptist Church of Philadelphia on December 10, 1763:

> In the name of the Lord Jesus, and according to the practice of his apostles towards persons chosen to the deaconship, I lay hands on you, my brother, whereby you are constituted or ordained a deacon of this church; installed in the office, and appointed and impowered [sic] to collect and receive her revenues; and to dispose thereof in providing for, and serving the Lord's-table; and providing for the table of the minister and the poor. . . .[28]

In 1774 Morgan Edwards, earliest historian of Baptists in America, described a deacon ordination which included a hymn about deacons. The first stanza related to the role of deacons in the Lord's Supper:

> The temple of the Lord are we
> His table here he hath,
> Which deacons serve, and serving, see
> Themselves advanc'd to good degree;
> And boldness in the faith.[29]

This is all well and good. The pressing question is whether contemporary Baptist deacons can move beyond the limited role in the Lord's Supper which their heritage has placed upon them. To do so seems imperative if deacons desire to raise the Lord's Supper to the peak level of worship that it should be, if they wish the Supper to be a resurgence of covenantal consecration rather than a meaningless worship experience, and if they want the meal to be a means of accenting the opportunities and duties of a regenerate church membership. In what ways can deacons (in cooperation with their pastors) bring a fresh and exciting thrust to the Lord's Supper?

First, deacons can share in a two-day retreat in which they focus entirely on their role in the Lord's Supper. In the retreat the pastor can lead a series of mini-studies on two main subjects. One is the biblical relationship between the Lord's Supper and a regenerate church membership. The other is the broad range of theological themes which are integral to a full understanding of the Supper. Deacons can use the retreat to do a lot of brainstorming on ways they can enhance the quality of Lord's Supper observances. Subjects for discussion might include ways to help a congregation prepare for the Supper (such as the creation of covenant meetings), ways to translate the biblical meanings of the Supper into worship practices which magnify the meanings, ways to encourage completely reverent responses to God during the meal, ways to distribute the bread and the cup which will distract the least from the congregation's awareness of the presence of God, and ways to follow up the Supper. Perhaps the deacons, led by their pastor, can climax the retreat with an actual observance of the Lord's Supper.

Second, in the week preceding the celebration of the Lord's Supper, the deacons can perform a telephone ministry whose goal is to alert every family in the church regarding the Supper about to take place and of the urgent need for every member to participate in it with a spirit of covenantal preparedness. When deacons call families, they can suggest that they read and study four key passages relating to the Lord's Supper (Matthew 26:26-28; Mark 14:22-24; Luke 22:17-20; 1 Corinthians 11:23-26) and that they pray that the Supper will have new meaning for them. If each deacon regularly provides various ministries to a specially assigned group of families in the church, then these are the families he or she should call. If a church does not have a deacon family ministry plan, the deacons can divide the church families into equal groups for the purpose of making the calls before this observance of the Lord's Supper. Perhaps this initial ministry to church families can lead to more extensive ministries by deacons in behalf of church members. The overall effect of a telephone ministry relating to the Lord's Supper will be to amplify the value of such worship for maintaining a regenerate church membership.

Third, deacons would do well, in cooperation with their pastor, to have in hand during the Lord's Supper cards which contain specific ministries needing to be performed by members of the congregation. The cards can include the names of persons who need to be visited—the homebound, the hospitalized, the bereaved, prisoners, those needing to know Christ as personal Savior, new residents of the community, and many others. Besides visitation, other ministries might be volunteer help with adult education classes, a clothing center, the mentally handicapped, international visitors or students, Bible schools for children on summer vacation, teaching positions in weekly church programs, or any one of many other such possibilities. The congregation should be alerted to the cards at the beginning of the Lord's Supper. Members should be encouraged to consider accepting a ministry as they experience the Supper and perceive through the meal the ultimate sacrifice which God made in their own behalf.

At the conclusion of the Lord's Supper, each deacon will personally select a ministry card in the presence of the congregation as an example for the other members. Members should then be invited to a specially designated area of the church building where the cards describing the ministries will be displayed. Each member who wishes, after examining several, will then select a card which describes a ministry he or she would particularly enjoy performing. Since each deacon will be responsible for a certain number of cards, his or her name will be on those specific ones. When a member completes a ministry, he or she will return the card to the appropriate deacon. Each deacon will keep a duplicate set of cards so that he or she will know when all the ministries he or she is coordinating are accomplished. When the Lord's Supper results in concrete spiritual ministries, the regenerate features of New Testament church membership will begin to thrive. In the process deacons will be living out the servant role which is their very reason for being.

From Theology to Practice

The Lord's Supper is a memorial which symbolizes the ultimate sacrifice of love and obedience by Jesus Christ in his death. More than that, "When the Lord's Supper is observed as it should be, it leads to fresh encounter between Christ and his people."[30] Remembrance, thanksgiving, worship, the renewal of allegiance to Christ, enjoyment of Christ's presence in the church, acknowledgment of Christ's death, and affirmation of hope in the Second Coming of Christ are all integral to the Supper and are all more than symbols.[31] The Lord's Supper is an ordinance of communicative action. God acts during the meal, and participants react. God uses no magic. The cup and loaf are that and no more. Still, the regular use of these New Testament worship aids both sharpens the participants' awareness of God's abiding love and heightens the urgency to respond to God without reservation.

For centuries Christians have tried to unravel the doctrinal substance of the Lord's Supper and have sought to give this substance practical expression in continuing celebration of the meal. One example of how the theology of the Supper was translated into a celebration of worship designed to meet a specific need occurred in the age of the Church Fathers. The people of the Greco-Roman milieu had an intense fear of demonic powers. As a missionary tool, therefore, the early church highlighted two aspects of Lord's Supper theology, namely, Christ's victory over the demonic and the eschatological hope extended by Christ, in observances of the meal. This enabled the Greco-Roman participants to have a sense of sharing in Christ's victory over the demonic, and it provided a message of hope for those fearful of demons. As the theology of the Lord's Supper was focused to meet a fundamental problem of early Christians, it can function today as a remedy for some of our own kind of problems. To illustrate, "The Lord's Supper, a simple action of eating and drinking together, could help to satisfy our modern longing for identity in the face of depersonalization." [32]

Pastors should make every effort to approach the Lord's Supper with an innovative spirit. Since many Baptist churches celebrate the Supper only four times each year, innovation ought not to be as difficult as it may first seem. Rather than be a highly predictable (and perhaps monotonous) service of worship preceded by little preparation by the Lord's Supper committee, the pastor, deacons, and church members, the Lord's Supper observance should be anticipated with careful planning and should have variety in its format and thrust. The goals of innovation are to magnify in clearly discernible form the New Testament meanings of the Supper, to give the Supper the biblical integrity it deserves among the fellowship of believers, and to strengthen the claims of Christ and the church upon each participant. Once achieved, these goals will lend genuine credibility to the regenerate nature of church membership.

A few alternative ways to celebrate the Lord's Supper are offered here. They are illustrative only. Many other possibilities exist, and each pastor will need to arrive at the approaches most meaningful in a particular situation. To begin with, a church may wish to emphasize that the Supper is the *Lord's* Supper. This can be done through visual imagery. The pulpit can be removed from the platform, and the Lord's Supper table can be placed on the platform. Three pulpit chairs can be placed behind the table facing the congregation. The two end chairs will be occupied by the pastor and an assisting deacon. The chair in the center remains vacant throughout the observance and has a small spotlight directed on it. With the lights in the building dimmed during the celebration, the empty chair surrounded by light represents the unseen Lord of the Supper. This approach accents the invisible presence of the Holy Spirit.

An optional approach to the Supper is to imitate the fact that there were twelve disciples in attendance at the original Supper. One church did this in the following manner.[33] After a Communion meditation led by the pastor, the deacons directed the members to the altar table in groups of twelve. A deacon at the table led each group in prayer. The pastor read brief passages of Scripture to each group, and a deacon served the bread and the cup to the twelve people. Successively, each group returned to their seats after a charge from the pastor. This approach will work best in a small- or medium-sized congregation. In a large church several groups of twelve can circle the altar table at the same time. Quiet and reverent movements by each group of twelve are essential in order not to distract from the atmosphere of worship. A basic advantage of this means of celebrating the Supper is that it requires a more active participation by members. Rather than have the loaf and the cup delivered to them by deacons while they sit passively, members are urged to make active, positive responses.

A third possible approach is to stress the fact that the Supper is family worship—meaning both the family of God and all eligible members of human families. This can be done in the fellowship hall of a church where tables and chairs are arranged in a large circle around the outer edges of the room. Chairs are on both sides of the tables. The room is aglow with candlelight. Soft meditative music fills the air. A Communion cup sits on the table in the front of each chair. One large uncut loaf of bread and two pitchers of beverage sit on the table at the pastor's seat. Members are encouraged in advance to enter this worship setting without conversation and to engage in silent meditation before the Supper actually begins. The Supper can then include a balanced use of prayers, Scriptures, music, and pastoral comments. Perhaps time can also be given for a few family members to share verbally some ways they feel that God is helping their family life to be more wholesome and meaningful. When the time comes to distribute the loaf, the pastor tears the loaf into two parts and passes one part to the right around the inside of the tables and the other around the outside. Each member pulls off a small piece as the loaf comes by. The two pitchers are then passed in like manner around the tables. Each member pours the beverage for the person sitting next in line. Worshiping around tables in this way highlights the themes of communion, fellowship, and family togetherness, which are so central to the Lord's Supper. This worship can end with all members holding hands and singing "Blest Be the Tie That Binds." As members leave the room without conversation, they are given the opportunity to contribute money for the poor.

Just as a baptismal pool occupies a prominent spot in the architectural design of most Baptist churches, the Lord's Supper table claims a conspicuous position in the arrangement of church furniture. The location of the table at the front and center of a congregation suggests that the Lord's Supper should be at the front and center of a congregation's worship experiences. Rather than being peripheral to true worship and an intrusion to normal patterns of worship, the Lord's Supper observance is the focal point around which all worship makes sense. For better or worse, the quality of Lord's Supper observances is the standard by which all other congregational worship is constructed. To treat the Lord's Supper casually is both an indication of the lack of depth in a church's worship habits and a tragic misunderstanding of the significance of this event in the life of a church. Let us treat this privilege as a sacred honor deserving the best preparation, the fullest participation, and the most complete subjugation to Christ. To accept this challenge humbly and to manage it creatively can be a real plus in a church's attempt to be thoroughly regenerate.

4

Church Membership in Discipline

Although church discipline has deep roots in the Bible and widespread precedents in Baptist history, such discipline has not been widely practiced among Baptists in America in the twentieth century. This trend has proved counterproductive to the growth of a regenerate church membership. Few concrete disciplines and covenantal expectations have been placed on church members by many congregations. Church members, therefore, have frequently responded both unenthusiastically and with a "take it or leave it attitude" to whatever membership responsibilities they have.

Among the overarching causes of disciplinary deterioration in Baptist life have been our failures to recognize the value of certain fundamental truths of our faith, to absorb these truths into the fabric of our being, and to implement the truths in lives of disciplined service and witness. These truths include the certainties that Christ is Lord, that personal commitment to Christ involves specific obligations to him and his church, and that the Bible is the authority for our church practices. Our understanding of the depths of these truths suffers immeasurably when we let church discipline slide into oblivion. A family, a civic club, a school, or even a nation will fail to meet major objectives without internal discipline. So will Baptist churches.

Fortunately, good news exists for those who will open their eyes and see. Many astute Christian thinkers have recently directed our thoughts to the potential and practical merits of church discipline. "The beginning of what appears to be a renewal of a committed, disciplined churchmanship is one of the facts of contemporary Christianity."[1] A purpose of this chapter is to identify ways in which this mounting thrust can support our efforts to sustain a regenerate church membership. Notice carefully the comments of these serious advocates of church discipline.

1. Dietrich Bonhoeffer:

> If the Church is to walk worthily of the gospel, part of its duty will be to maintain ecclesiastical discipline. Sanctification means driving out the world from the Church as well as separating the Church from the world.[2]

2. Findley B. Edge:

> [A] ... major innovation that will be necessary in the life of the church if we are to approach the ideal of a regenerate church member involves the practice of Christian discipline.[3]

3. Norman H. Maring and Winthrop S. Hudson:

> Many influences have brought about a relaxation of standards for admission to church membership and permitted church members to treat their responsibilities lightly. It we are to take seriously the idea of regenerate churches . . . some form of discipline would need to be reinstituted.[4]

4. J. Herbert Gilmore, Jr.:

> The church is always one generation away from paganism. It does not necessarily follow that our sons and daughters will embrace the faith and convictions of their parents. This points up the necessity of the church being a disciplined organism that may transmit authentic faith from one generation to another.[5]

The time is ripe for a disciplinary reawakening in Baptist life. Many churches are responding favorably to the incorporation of covenantal disciplines into their patterns of worship, witness, service, giving, and learning. "Discipline" has its root in the Latin verb *discere*, "to learn." Many churches are creatively implementing the learning function of the disciplinary process. These churches are making excellent application of the dual educational emphases which lie at the heart of church discipline. First, they are using formative discipline, which includes active participation in Christian ministries and positive instruction in the truth of God and the Bible. Second, these churches are using reformative discipline, a form of instruction focusing on remedial correction for problems of conduct, doctrinal deviations, and serious sins.

Formative discipline without reformative discipline encourages church members to accede to their covenantal duties but lacks the power to deal effectively and redemptively with covenantal offenders. Reformative discipline without formative discipline results in a legalistic, punitive, and negative approach to discipline that does more harm than good. Joined in a common bond, the two types of discipline promote the healthiest kind of membership education and integrity. The goal of discipline is to help church members learn that New Testament standards must be maintained.

Discipline is learning. Inactive church members, nonresident members, and even faithful church participants need to continue their education in the fundamentals of church membership. To facilitate this education, this chapter will first describe the important role of discipline in Scripture and in Baptist history. A knowledge of biblical authority for discipline and a demonstration of its historical effectiveness are essential to a wholesome confrontation with the disciplinary gap so widely prevalent in Baptist churches today. Once these points are made, suggestions will be offered for a contemporary application of church discipline in Baptist life.

DISCIPLINE IN THE BIBLE

Many readers will be astounded to see that there is so much biblical material on discipline. We have too readily ignored the teaching of Scripture related to discipline.[6] Although Baptists identify the Bible as the ultimate written authority for their faith and practice, they frequently overlook the fact that disciplinary concerns occupy a prominent role in Scripture. Far less material exists on such subjects as deacons and ordination, but we do not hesitate to ascribe paramount importance to these matters in our church life. Perhaps a closer look at passages on discipline will bring into sharper focus the disciplinary possibilities in churches today.

We must examine the New Testament for ideas about church discipline, but we must first look briefly at the pre-Christian background concepts about discipline in both the Old Testament and the Dead Sea Scrolls. In the Old Testament, formative discipline took many shapes. One was regular instruction in and public reading of the Law (Deuteronomy 6:1-9; 2 Kings 23:1-3). Another was the regular celebration of religious feasts and other spiritual observances (Exodus 16:22-30; Leviticus 23). Still another was the powerful preaching of the prophets, although this preaching often took a reformative shape as well.

Reformative discipline was a vital Old Testament practice. The breaking of covenantal vows routinely resulted in the administration of discipline (Leviticus 26:14ff., 23ff.; Deuteronomy 17:2ff.; 29:25-28; 31:16-17; Joshua 7:10-15; 23:16; Judges 2:20-23). Several types of discipline existed.[7] Divine intervention through nature was the form of discipline applied to the Korah-Dathan-Abiram revolt (Numbers 16, especially vv. 31-35). Discipline through human instrumentality occurred in the case of the idolatry of the golden calf (Exodus 32, especially vv. 25-29, 35). Admission into the assembly of the Lord was delayed or denied those guilty of certain sexual offenses or those among Israel's enemies (Deuteronomy 23:1-8). Postexilic discipline included forfeiture of property and banning from "the congregation of the exiles" for those who did not attend Ezra's reform assembly. The goal of this discipline was to bring about separation from foreign wives (Ezra 9:1f.; 10, especially v. 8,). Capital punishment was administered for the most severe infractions. Examples were murder (Exodus 21:12), striking or cursing one's father or mother (Exodus 21:15, 17), stealing a Hebrew and selling him into slavery (Exodus 21:16), fornication with a beast (Exodus 22:19), and sacrificing to any god except the Lord (Exodus 22:20). Death in these instances was usually by stoning.

The Essenes at Qumran had a rigid disciplinary system. According to the Dead Sea Scrolls, initiation into the Qumran community involved the acceptance of a covenant to God and the community by each applicant. The covenanters at Qumran were disciplined when they failed to keep their pledge or when they violated the rules of the community. The usual form of discipline was separation from the community for a certain number of days or months, depending on the nature of the infraction. The most stringent form of discipline was exclusion for life, which resulted when a member of the community was found guilty of cursing God, complaining against the community, or lapsing after being in the community for ten years.[8]

Formative disciplinary teachings permeate the New Testament. The Sermon on the Mount offers positive guidance in Christian discipleship and provides a structure for the ethics of New Testament churches. The exemplary lives of Jesus, Paul, and others present spiritual qualities worthy of imitation. The letters of Paul to churches he helped establish gave nurturing encouragement to struggling congregations. Such preventive discipline was designed to preclude the need for corrective action by early Christian churches. The bulk of the discipline in the New Testament, as well as the Old, focuses on formative concepts.

Still, the New Testament says much about reformative, remedial, and corrective discipline. These are passages which Baptists of the twentieth century are largely failing to implement. What are these passages and what do they say? One way to approach these questions is to examine selected passages. Probably the most familiar words of Jesus on reformative discipline are the following:

> "If your brother sins against you, go and tell him his fault, between you and him alone. If he listens to you, you have gained your brother. But if he does not listen, take one or two others along with you, that every word may be confirmed by the evidence of two or three witnesses. If he refuses to listen to them, tell it to the church; and if he refuses to listen even to the church, let him be to you as a Gentile and a tax collector" (Matthew 18:15-17).

In this passage Jesus prescribes several steps in the disciplinary process. Reconciliation is the goal of each step. The private approach, the committee approach, and then the congregational approach are arranged purposefully in this particular order. This sequence makes it possible for the least number of people to know about one's covenantal violation. It also provides an offender with several opportunities to become repentant and reconciled and gives him or her time to think through the problem carefully. Further, the sequence prevents the total congregation from becoming involved in covenantal violations which can be handled more effectively by individual members or groups of members. However, the sequence also makes clear that the ultimate responsibility for disciplinary measures resides with the total congregation when covenantal problems cannot be worked out in any other way. The idea of treating an offender as "a Gentile and a tax collector" does not necessarily imply an act of excommunication. Rather, it can imply the simple recognition that an offender has excommunicated himself or herself. Since Jesus ate with Gentiles and tax collectors, the church is still to make available its spiritual resources to those refusing to respond to the discipline of the church.

In the Acts of the Apostles, Ananias and Sapphira fell victim not to discipline administered by the church but to punishment resulting from divine action (5:1-11). This account vividly shows the strictness of early Christian discipline. Ananias and Sapphira placed themselves outside the fellowship of the church through deception of the fellowship and a hypocritical spirit of sacrifice.

Also in Acts, Simon Magus met discipline before Peter (8:18-24), and Elymas the magician met discipline before Paul (13:8-11). Simon Magus sought the power of the Holy Spirit for monetary reasons, and Peter pronounced a malediction on him and his money. Elymas, a non-Christian, tried to divert Sergius Paulus, proconsul at Paphos, from the word of God being taught by Barnabas and Paul. The discipline meted out to Elymas was temporary blindness. The discipline of the early Christian church was so alive that church leaders, as in these two instances, occasionally applied it to persons not in the church who were exerting negative influences upon the Christian community. Discipline was tough in both these instances.

The writings of Paul contain many references to discipline. Paul admonishes the Romans to avoid those who cause dissension in their opposition to Christian doctrine (Romans 16:17). A highly instructive passage on Christian discipline is 1 Corinthians 5:1-13, which focuses on a case of incest. Besides showing that discipline is to be strict (v. 13), the passage also deals with the dual motivation of discipline—to preserve the church (vv. 6-8) and to restore the errant member (v. 5). A passage in Second Corinthians (2:5-11), which possibly relates to the incest passage in 1 Corinthians 5, teaches that forgiveness is central to discipline. Because an erring brother has repented, the Corinthians are to forgive him so that Satan will gain no advantage over them.

Paul's censure of Peter (Galatians 2:11f.) shows that even

Christian leaders are within the scope of the church's discipline. Paul cautions the Thessalonians to "admonish" (1 Thessalonians 5:14) and even to "keep away from" (2 Thessalonians 3:6) idle Christians. In a doctrinal dispute in which Hymenaeus, Alexander, and Philetus disturb the faith of certain believers, Paul writes, "I have delivered [them] to Satan that they may learn not to blaspheme" (1 Timothy 1:20; see also 2 Timothy 2:16-18). This seems to suggest a form of excommunication with the hope of restoration. Paul says further in Titus that Judaizers are to be rebuked sharply "that they may be sound in the faith" (1:13); that exhortation and reproof are to be done with authority so that such discipline will not be disregarded (2:15); and that a disruptive person who has received one or two warnings should be avoided since such a one is self-condemned (3:10-11).

Non-Pauline epistles give similar attention to discipline. Hebrews contains several extremely important references to discipline in the early church (3:12-16; 6:4-8; 10:26-30; 12:5-17). A major goal of Hebrews is to instruct those about to abandon the faith. James writes that the recovery of a brother from sinful habits is a desirable objective (5:19-20). False teachers are to be avoided (2 Peter 2:1-2, 9-19; 1 John 4:1-3; 2 John 7:11; Jude 4, 8-23). Third John indicates that Diotrephes has misused discipline (9-10). The book of Revelation cautions the churches of Asia against false teachers (2:14-16, 20-26).

Regardless of how Baptists interpret Scripture, we cannot justify our prevalent tendency to bypass those passages relating to discipline. We must acknowledge that material on this subject is integral to the Bible, and we must come to terms with it. The New Testament is clear: offenses against God and/or the church are not to be overlooked. To pretend that serious offenses do not exist is a slap in the face of disciplinary patterns advocated by Jesus and New Testament leaders and writers.

The Bible does not call for a system of legalistic ethics. Instead, it recommends a functional combination of discipline and forgiveness. Discipline without forgiveness is disruptive of church fellowship and harmful to an erring member. Forgiveness without discipline is a toleration of sin which can jeopardize the whole concept of a regenerate church membership. Working together, discipline and forgiveness can bring integrity, health, and vigor to congregational life.

Each Baptist church will need to come to its own integrated understanding of how to implement the style of church discipline presented in the New Testament. Understanding must be followed by application. Application must be constant and equitable in order to be successful. Remember: love, not vengeance, is discipline's foundation. God, the church, and erring members will benefit if discipline follows New Testament guidelines; and the doctrine of a regenerate membership will begin to receive more adequate attention.

DISCIPLINE AND COVENANTS: RELATIONSHIP AND NEGLECT

"The motif of responsible discipline in the Christian community has been repeatedly emphasized during Christian history."[9] Baptist history, especially that of the nineteenth century and earlier, is replete with examples of disciplinary action by churches. Baptist church discipline has been a natural corollary of church covenants. Preventive discipline has been the attempt to practice the individual disciplines comprising church covenants. Corrective discipline has been the effort to deal constructively with covenantal violators, although the results have sometimes not been very constructive.

The twentieth century has witnessed a decline in discipline in Baptist life. Nevertheless, some churches and writers have made significant attempts in recent years to reverse this trend. Before giving suggestions for a renewed and modified application of discipline in churches today, a brief survey of disciplinary patterns in our Baptist past both will show that discipline has been an important feature of our heritage and will reveal precedents for using it today. Many Baptists have either forgotten or never become acquainted with the valuable role discipline has played in Baptist history.

Although there is some question about the extent to which Anabaptists influenced early English Baptists, both groups incorporated disciplinary themes directly into the heart of their church covenants.

The Anabaptist view of the church covenant enforced vigorous internal discipline, in imitation of Christ, including baptism, the Lord's Supper, a ban against association with unbelievers, non-resistance, non-swearing, cross-bearing in martyrdom, and a vocation for each member in carrying out the Great Commission.[10]

Several seventeenth-century English Baptist churches included disciplinary statements in their covenants. One such church was that in Amersham, whose covenant of 1675 stated that: (1) each member must be willing to submit to church discipline, should this become necessary; (2) the disciplinary pattern to be followed was that specified in Matthew 18:15-17; (3) the purpose of discipline was to "gaine a sole [soul] to God and hide a Multitude of sin"; and (4) anyone who brought a fake charge against another member would himself be disciplined.[11]

The covenant published in 1697 by Elias Keach, a well-known London pastor, included the pledge that the covenanters would submit "to the Discipline of the Gospel, and all Holy Duties required of a People in such a spiritual Relation."[12] The covenant then listed eight categories of duties. This statement of covenantal discipline was significant in that it later attained prominence in America. The Welsh Tract Baptist Church in Delaware, which adopted this covenant in 1710, became the principal means of introducing church covenants to the Baptists in the Middle Colonies.[13] This church did not hesitate to exercise its disciplinary prerogative. Exclusion from membership for covenant breaking was the judgment laid at times upon several members.[14] This was a common practice among Baptist churches in colonial America.

Besides appearing in church covenants, early Baptist statements on discipline also existed in formal disciplinary treatises and in confessions of faith.[15] The two most important disciplinary treatises by Baptists prior to the American Revolution were the *Short Treatise,* published by the Philadelphia Association in 1743, and *A Summary of Church Discipline,* published by the Charleston Association in 1774. These two documents achieved wide influence among eighteenth-century Baptists. A confession of faith which included a disciplinary emphasis was that adopted by the Sandy Creek Association in North Carolina in 1816. This confession described a church as "a congregation of faithful persons, who have obtained fellowship with each other, and have given themselves up to the Lord and one another; having agreed to keep up a godly discipline, according to the rules of the Gospel."[16]

In 1897, Edwin C. Dargan, professor of homiletics and ecclesiology at the Southern Baptist Theological Seminary in Louisville, Kentucky, wrote, "It is a mournful fact that in many of our churches to-day apostolic discipline may be said not to exist.

. . ."[17] At least two reasons likely accounted for the decline of discipline which Dargan sensed at the end of the nineteenth century and which has continued into the 1970s, thus impeding the efforts to sustain a regenerate church membership.

First, the decline of discipline, which was accompanied by a decline in church covenants, in the final years of the nineteenth century may have been associated with a general secularizing process which was capturing American religion and culture. The lowering of standards of conduct in public and private life as a result of the Civil War, the tremendous increase in the wealth of the United States from about 1880 onwards, and the astonishing growth of cities in the 1880s[18] may all have contributed to the depreciation of discipline and covenants.

Second, and equally as important, the decline has been a reaction to the legalistic use of discipline and covenants. Baptists have responded negatively and justifiably to such an idea as that of Soares when he claimed in his church manual: "It is the duty of every member of the church to perform faithfully the letter and spirit of its covenant. . . ."[19] The problem is that Baptists have overreacted to the extent that they have often rejected all the potential values of discipline and covenants.

A helpful way to see how Baptist church discipline became so legalistic is to look both at disciplinary patterns on the American frontier and at the disciplinary thrusts in Baptist church manuals of the nineteenth and twentieth centuries. Frontier Baptists maintained an extremely tight relationship between church covenants and church discipline. The probable reason was that the untamed character of frontier life required the churches to employ special taming devices. Discipline resulted from the failure to adhere closely to one's covenantal promises. In the Mays Lick, Kentucky, Baptist Church, a covenant was read often, and "it was insisted upon and emphasized by strict discipline that every member should strive to conform his life to his covenant."[20] The discipline for a large variety of offenses was administered rigidly and impartially in this and other frontier churches.

The minutes of Baptist churches on the early American frontier clearly revealed the legalistic nature of discipline. Disciplinary matters so dominated church covenant meetings that the minutes were similar to the case proceedings on the docket of a civil court. For example, on the first Saturday in October, 1821, the New

Liberty Church in Kentucky acted upon ten items of business. Nine of these concerned disciplinary matters, and seven members were excluded from the church.[21] One researcher demonstrated the legalistic and harsh scope of discipline administered by five frontier Baptist churches in Kentucky from 1781 to 1860. Of 1,636 offenses dealt with by the churches in this period, 821, or just over one-half, resulted in exclusions from membership.[22]

The kinds of offenses which led to exclusions quickly show the legalistic character of frontier Baptist discipline. In five frontier churches in Kentucky between 1800 and 1860, the following were among the reasons listed in the minutes of the churches as to why members were excluded: stealing, beating one's wife, telling lies, mistreating another person, gambling, cursing, threatening suicide, drinking too much, fighting, living in adultery, being pregnant outside of marriage, striking one's father-in-law, refusing to attend church, dancing, moving from the state without applying for a letter of dismission, bad conduct in a church meeting, refusing to pay a debt, attending a horse race, denying the faith and doctrine of the church, misrepresenting persons in the church to the grand jury in the county, violating the rules of the church, playing cards and billiards, taking out a lawsuit against another person, murder, and betting.[23]

Many Baptist church manuals, especially of the nineteenth and early twentieth centuries, stood rather solidly behind the idea that violations of one's covenantal agreements with one's church should be countered with disciplinary action. A typical assertion in these manuals was that "[a church] has the right to require of all its members a punctual performance of all the duties prescribed in the church covenant and in the Word of God, and to call them to account for neglect or violation."[24]

Several manual writers associated covenants primarily with corrective discipline. The net result was an overidentification of church covenants with the negative side of discipline. This identification was the inevitable consequence of viewing covenants as legal documents. This assignment of a legalistic quality to the contents of covenants negated much of the value which might have accrued from preventive discipline. Punishment for covenantal violations received disproportionate attention in some church manuals in comparison with any kind of positive stress on the therapeutic possibilities inherent in meaningful covenanting.

The legalistic approach to discipline created opposition to the whole concept of discipline among Baptists, and the opposition persists even today. Legalism tagged discipline with several negative features. Standards of morality were black and white; an action was either right or wrong. Thus, a negative ethic tended to dominate religious life. This ethical life-style resulted in a disciplinary theory which implied that Christianity was more restricting than liberating.

Churches which practiced legalistic discipline often made no serious efforts to reclaim persons whom they excluded from membership. The churches were evidently so preoccupied with ridding themselves of the morally weak that they failed to develop a responsible ministry to the persons whom they expelled. As a result, a high percentage of the persons excluded from membership were never restored.

The churches with extremely rigid discipline were apparently more interested in maintaining corporate self-purification than they were in offering spiritual therapy to individual members with problems. The churches placed so much emphasis on preserving their institutional sanctity that they had little tolerance for individual deviations from the established norms. Such intolerance grew out of weak concepts of personhood and the church. In their efforts to keep themselves holy by excluding undesirable members, churches failed to realize the sinful nature of the members who did the excluding. The doctrine of original sin and the ambiguities of certain moral predicaments received little attention in exclusion procedures.

Legalistically oriented churches gave far more attention to the corrective, punitive, and remedial aspects of discipline than they did to the constructive, preventive, and formative aspects. Consequently, there was a rather sizable failure to meet the pastoral needs of members. When churches excluded members for premarital pregnancies, divorce, and other family problems, the churches intensified the problems of these members rather than offer help for them.

SUGGESTIONS FOR CONTEMPORARY APPLICATION

Historically, Baptists have tended to maintain a close relationship between church covenants and church discipline. Too frequently, covenants have been associated with a negative kind of discipline. The stress has been on punishing members for covenantal infractions. A depreciation of the values of church covenants and church discipline has resulted. In one sense the current aversion to corrective church discipline is understandable. Baptists may simply be reacting to disciplinary extremes which have existed in the past. The other side of the story is that the present disciplinary laxness may be a subtle technique for evading the reality of sin in institutional church life and for justifying an ethical system that falls short of New Testament standards. Whatever the case, the regenerate nature of the church suffers when the church fails to confront the serious sins of its members with compassionate censure. Church discipline in its preventive and corrective applications is an essential guardian of the regenerate quality of church life.

Church covenants fit more readily into a pastoral setting when the authority behind them is not that of a disciplinary "watchdog" but that of a caring and supportive congregation. The disciplinary value of a covenant exists mainly in an alliance with preventive and formative discipline rather than with corrective and punitive discipline. Ideally, a covenant guides church members into spiritual and ethical adventures which are positive expressions of their faith. The covenantal practice of providing disciplines by which church members can live out their commitments most meaningfully must be restored. All possible assistance must be given to the renewal of a responsible approach to discipline in Baptist churches. Nine suggestions will be offered that may be helpful for a contemporary understanding and application of church discipline in Baptist life.

1. Come to terms with frequently raised objections to a disciplined church membership. One writer described and countered ten such objections.[25] Discipline, according to these objections, is legalistic, denies freedom, deters growth, creates exclusiveness, opposes evangelism, is unacceptable to church members, is idealistic and not practical, causes self-righteousness, offends errant members, and is judgmental. The last objection fails to recognize that Jesus did not condemn all judging but rather the hypocritical variety (Matthew 6:5; John 8:7).

In reality healthy church discipline can be liberating, an extension and control of freedom, a stimulus to growth, a cultivator of inclusiveness characterized by moral and spiritual integrity, a tool for quality control in membership, a source of humility, and a redemptive factor for wayward members. Objections to church discipline are many, but the disciplinary demands of the New Testament must take precedence over current aversions to this biblical practice. In an age when church membership duties, covenant obligations, and individual and social morality are viewed and practiced far too casually, church discipline (preventive and corrective) is completely in order as a means of helping to produce a wholly regenerate church membership—objections to the contrary.

2. Avoid the extreme of converting church discipline into legalism. "Probably the greatest problem in the recovery [of discipline] is the avoidance of a neo-Pharisaic legalism." [26] Although church discipline has been an important feature of Baptist history, it has sometimes assumed unnecessarily rigid applications. This has resulted in a codification of sins with appropriate retribution for each. A full dose of grace, redemption, and forgiveness must be swallowed by any church desiring to let discipline be a meaningful part of its effort to be regenerate.

Paul wrote toward the end of Second Thessalonians: "If any one refuses to obey what we say in this letter, note that man, and have nothing to do with him, that he may be ashamed. Do not look on him as an enemy, but warn him as a brother" (3:14-15). Paul recommended discipline but not with a highly legal and once-for-all attitude. Fellow Christians are brothers and sisters in the faith even after subjection to the corrective admonishment of a congregation. Love, not legality, is to be the driving force behind church discipline.

3. Take discipline seriously in order to make it successful. "Those who would lead in the renewal of discipline must be thoroughly convinced of its terrible urgency. Both positive nurture and negative censures . . . are needed." [27] It is easy to criticize Baptists of the past for using discipline that seems overly harsh by today's standards, but we cannot deny that these Baptists took discipline seriously. Church membership is a privilege which necessitates responsible moral living. To violate a covenantal agreement with one's church on a regular basis means that a member should be reminded of his or her duties by the church. Nothing can be more commendable than for a church to cultivate disciplinary patterns designed to encourage the consistent practice

of biblical ethics in all phases of the lives of all the congregation.

4. State the church's disciplines in a written covenant. Faithful participation in worship, prayer, Bible study, and the giving of money, service, and witness are the kinds of nurturing disciplines which can comprise a good covenant. These disciplines are placed before the membership in baptism, the Lord's Supper, preaching, and other settings. The disciplines will eventually occupy a place of prominence in the lives of members. The implementation of any disciplinary process must be preceded by a careful evaluation of just what a church's disciplines will be. If the disciplines are worth having, they are worth penning in a formal document that receives wide dissemination and a high spiritual status among a fellowship of believers.

5. Construct church discipline on a solidly biblical basis. Although there is a close bond between discipline and church covenants, a church covenant is not in itself a legitimate basis for administering corrective church discipline. In no sense does a covenant supplant the disciplinary foundations and procedures in the New Testament. Rather, the constructive function of a covenant is to preclude the necessity of reformative discipline by magnifying biblical principles which can lead church members into spiritually and morally formative Christian living and actions. One scholar clearly depicted the relationship between church discipline and the biblical authority underlying a covenant. He wrote that

> church discipline is not to be decided by the articles of the Covenant, but by the biblical principles which may be expressed in the Covenant. To use the Church Covenant as a measuring rod for church discipline is to short circuit biblical authority.[28]

6. View discipline as the task of the entire congregation. Discipline is not simply the work of the pastor or the deacons. Every member performs a ministry of influence through fulfilling covenantal pledges. This exemplary life-style can easily affect others in a remarkably helpful way and thereby express preventive discipline at its best. Even corrective discipline, following the guidelines posited in Matthew 18:15-17, may require congregational involvement. The best kind of church discipline exists in the genuinely sensitive concern which members continually have for one another. A congregation can expect to achieve a fully regenerate status only if all its members are willing to sponsor and

live by the personal and corporate disciplines of the church.

7. Place primary emphasis on the formative phase of discipline, rather than on the reformative. The fundamental goal of discipline is to keep church members biblically sound, morally upright, and spiritually strong. The converse ideal is to keep church members from lapsing into heresy, immorality, and opposition to God and God's people. This goal can be achieved through serious covenantal instruction, vigorous Bible teaching programs, substantive preaching, and attention to such basic disciplines as regular church attendance, generous financial offerings, and participation in ministries. A reasonable goal is for formative discipline to be so effective that reformative discipline is not needed.

8. Assist a wayward member best by helping him or her solve the problem, not by excluding him or her. Exclusions may still be necessary, however, in cases of deliberate hostility to the church and its spiritual welfare. A punitive application of corrective discipline must be precluded by the candid acknowledgment that all people possess a sinful nature. The absence of church discipline today should not be countered by a return to the harsh discipline that once existed. Middle ground needs to be sought. Although churches are striving for maturity and perfection, their members are redeemed sinners. The practice of discipline is essential, but it needs to be conditioned by the wisdom of the statement possibly made by Jesus (the account does not exist in some ancient texts) in addressing the scribes and Pharisees who believed that a woman caught in adultery should be stoned: "Let him who is without sin among you be the first to throw a stone at her" (John 8:7). Caring concern, not illegitimate judging, must characterize Baptist church discipline.

9. Apply church discipline with therapeutic intentions and with the hope of redemption and reconciliation, or not at all. The motivation behind discipline is of primary importance. Discipline cannot become a medium for venting personal hostilities through manufacturing false evidence against specific persons. Instead, "if a man is overtaken in any trespass, you who are spiritual should restore him in a spirit of gentleness" (Galatians 6:1). Discipline is a means of reinforcing the teachings of Jesus and the covenantal obligations of church members. Discipline can best focus on alleviating individual need and not on a superficial preservation of

the sanctity of the church. If the latter emphasis prevails, the entire congregation may need internal disciplining. If the former emphasis is at play, the church is meeting an essential responsibility to its members.

To conclude, a response will be made to a few frequently raised questions about corrective church discipline. First, who decides when discipline is necessary? This depends entirely on the situation. Matthew 18:15 shows that a single Christian can decide. Matthew 18:16 reveals that a group of church members can make the decision. Matthew 18:17 indicates that an entire church can launch disciplinary initiative. One possible guideline for determining who makes the decision about discipline is this: the larger the number of church members directly affected by a situation requiring discipline, the more members should be involved in saying that discipline ought to occur. If a member maligns the character of another member unjustifiably, then the maligned member has the right as an individual personally to admonish and seek reconciliation from his or her attacker. If a member maligns the character of a whole group within a church, then the group can ethically take steps to deal with the offender. If a pastor or other staff member becomes entangled in a serious moral blunder which renders his or her ministry ineffective, then an entire congregation may need to decide in unity that discipline is in order.

Second, who actually does the disciplining and what are the steps involved in carrying it out? Normally, discipline should be done by those persons who decide that it ought to be done. A member may censure another member in a home or in any other location, as long as he or she makes every effort to keep the censure as private as possible. A group may also perform discipline in any suitable setting and will try to refrain from sharing the details of such an encounter with other church members or with outsiders. An entire congregation probably does best to discipline members in church business meetings. However, flagrant violations of moral conduct or doctrinal heresies may demand more immediate action in special congregational meetings.

In carrying out congregational discipline in a business meeting, the situation requiring discipline should be described to the congregation in general terms by the pastor or some other member only after careful consideration has been given by the church staff and other members to the merits of bringing the case to the church.

The names of guilty members should be included in the report, along with a recommendation as to what disciplinary action should be pursued. If the guilty members are present, they should be asked to leave the room during the discussion and vote. Once the disciplinary action is decided, the church will want to make every effort to share the action with the guilty members in a way that will not cause inordinate embarrassment. Perhaps the best way is for the pastor to share it privately when the meeting is over. Guilty persons not present may properly be informed by a personal visit, a telephone call, or a personal letter from the pastor in behalf of the church. In each case the desire of the church for reconciliation should accompany the discipline of the church.

Three points are worth remembering in employing corrective discipline. First, church members who have knowledge of disciplinary proceedings against other members should not gossip about the details and risk unnecessary harm to the reputation of disciplined members. Second, a disciplinary problem should be resolved at an early level when as few people as possible are involved. Third, each church will need to decide for itself the offenses which it believes deserve discipline. The Bible must be the basis for making this decision.

5

Church Membership in
Witness

Evangelism is another feature of Baptist life which has a close relationship with the concept of a regenerate church membership. Church members who have responded to the good news about Christ and experienced regeneration by the Holy Spirit joyfully share the message of Christian redemption with people who need to hear it. The teachings of Jesus capsulized in Matthew 28:19-20 and reflected in his ministry throughout the Gospels show that every Christian is to bear witness to his or her faith. In the words of the 1963 Statement of Faith of the Southern Baptist Convention, "It is the duty of every child of God to seek constantly to win the lost to Christ by personal effort and by all other methods in harmony with the gospel of Christ." [1]

The primary problem Baptists face with evangelism is that not enough church members are doing it. To illustrate, in Southern Baptist life it takes about thirty church members to secure each baptism that occurs.[2] Further, recent statistics show that over 30 percent of those baptized are eleven years old or younger.[3] Most of these youngsters probably do not require a tremendous amount of persuasion to make their decisions for Christ. Baptists do face other problems with evangelism, such as the occasional use of manipulative tactics, the growing tendency to seek the conversion of preschoolers, and criticisms directed by nonwitnessing Baptists toward the strategies and techniques of church members who are attempting to perform genuine and legitimate evangelism. These problems are serious but not nearly so dangerous as the failure of thousands of Baptists to express verbally a responsible testimony.

Cecil E. Sherman, pastor of the First Baptist Church of Asheville, North Carolina, wrote prophetically when he both encouraged his congregation to prepare for a Billy Graham evangelistic crusade in Asheville and tackled nonwitnessing critics of mass evangelism:

> We can "talk up" this crusade. One of the most devastating problems we have in this kind of meeting is the negative talk of some Christians. I have heard this talk. It takes all shapes. Some do not trust "mass evangelism." Others have some complaint about the style. On and on this kind of talk can go. You may have a tendency to listen to this sort of talk. But here is my only comment about this kind of talk. Are the people who are talking doing any kind of evangelism? The Bible tells us to be witnesses (Acts 1:8). Most of us are worship attenders, money givers, and sometimes we are ministry people. Our greatest failing comes in the area of witness.[4]

Even though the absence of sincere witnessing in much Baptist life is the fundamental problem with Baptist evangelism and produces entirely negative results, the other problems must also be reckoned with. If Baptists employ shallow evangelistic practices, if they bear witness to their faith primarily to record statistical successes, or if they try to make Christians of children too young to have even the remotest understanding of what Christianity is about, then the regenerate texture of church life will suffer. In these cases the best results that can be expected, apart from minimal exceptions, are strong opposition to the witnessing patterns of the church by non-Christians, church membership rolls filled with people who really find little meaning in their status as Christians and church members, and young people growing up with a variety of reservations about the value of the new birth in Christ they supposedly experienced as young children. A regenerate church membership does not have a chance to survive if these kinds of evangelistic results become cumulative over the decades.

EVANGELISM AND REGENERATE CHURCH MEMBERSHIP

Positively, if Baptist evangelism focuses on assisting non-

Christians in a penetrating search for spiritual meaning, if it acknowledges the full worth of every person in the sight of God, if it recognizes that children in the infant stage and just beyond are not accountable for sins, if it resorts to biblical rather than manipulative tactics, and, most of all, if it achieves widespread participation and support by a vast majority of church members, then it can increase its contribution to potential Christians and to the quality of church life. Church members tend to perpetuate Christians of their own kind. The evangelistic mode and model of a Baptist church in this decade will likely be imitated by those members leading out in the witnessing ministry of the same church in the next decade. Since the evangelistic style of a church will either add to or detract from the church's regenerate features, the evangelism actually used must submit to creative encounter with New Testament patterns and must judge the effectiveness of its results by the level of sustained commitment which new Christians have for Christ and the church.

What is evangelism? "Evangelism means essentially the outreach of the church to persuade men [and women] to acknowledge Jesus Christ as Savior and to obey him as Lord in the totality of their lives."[5] What is the relationship between evangelism and a regenerate church membership? The regenerated Christian who has experienced the good news of Christ through the Holy Spirit discovers immediately that a high priority of the new life in Christ is to share the good news with others. Thus, evangelism is integral to the life of a church. A regenerate church membership can rise or fall on the basis of whether church members do evangelism and on the quality of such witness. Christ mandated the church to witness vigorously. When the church does less, it robs itself both of a reason for being and of a ministry of love.

A church should use whatever legitimate means are required to encourage all its members to engage in healthy forms of evangelism. The goal of this chapter is to provide a framework of selected principles and suggestions which a church can use to develop and support a style of evangelism which is biblically based, God-oriented, person-centered, and functionally practical and appealing. Since countless volumes have been published on evangelism, the guidelines offered here are not so original that they fail to take advantage of the accumulated evangelistic wisdom of the past. Hopefully, a fresh wording, a new sequence of ideas, a special combination of illustrations from the Bible and Baptist history, a view of Christian witnessing in the context of a regenerate church membership, and a genuine prayer that we will take our evangelistic tasks more earnestly will give the chapter some measure of worth.

EVANGELISM IS THE DUTY AND PRIVILEGE OF ALL CHURCH MEMBERS

The word in the Greek New Testament from which "evangelism" is derived literally means "good news" or "gospel." The basic content of the "good news" is Christ, his words and his acts. Evangelism focuses on a fundamental role of the Christian community—sharing the "good news." The mandate for bearing a witness begins with the life, death, and resurrection of Christ. The mandate applies to all believers. Acts 1:8 describes the apostles as "witnesses." Acts 13:31 describes the Christian community at large as "witnesses." The concept of witnesses bearing the gospel of Christ permeates Acts. The Day of Pentecost symbolized the empowering of the followers of Christ for telling the world about Christ. The reality of the Holy Spirit gives contemporary disciples the same power for sharing the gospel.

Witnessing for Christ is an essential task of all Christians. Avoidance of this task by Baptists is as widespread as acceptance of it. Many reasons (excuses) pile up for our failure to take evangelistic opportunities seriously. A major problem which has evolved is that of letting paid professionals (church staffs, missionaries, and general evangelists) do evangelism. When the apostle Paul writes, "And his gifts were that some should be apostles, some prophets, some evangelists, some pastors and teachers" (Ephesians 4:11), many interpret this to mean that sharing the good news belongs primarily to Christian leaders who have special responsibilities in this regard. Actually, this view is more of a rationalization than a bona fide interpretation. Bearing a responsible witness is common to all the persons listed in Ephesians 4:11, as well as to all Christians not listed.

The recovery of an approach to evangelism that makes this work an inclusive function of an entire church membership can come partly by taking a new look at the New Testament idea of the priesthood of believers. If this concept means anything, it suggests that Christians have a unique privilege to imitate the witness to God performed by Christ. The reason Christians are tagged a "royal priesthood" in 1 Peter 2:9 is "that you may declare the wonderful deeds of him who called you out of darkness into his marvelous light." This verse implies undeniably that making known the presence and love of Christ to non-Christians is vital to the spiritual maturity of Christian priests. The priesthood of believers is more than a sterile doctrine or a sign of token status or favor with God; it is the theological backbone of evangelism by all Christians.

If 1 Peter 2:9 is not adequately convincing, consider Revelation 1:4-6. These verses describe Jesus Christ as "the faithful witness" who "has freed us from our sins by his blood and made us a kingdom, priests to his God and Father." Implicit in this assertion is that imitation of Christ requires that we be witnesses too. John, the writer of Revelation, did not simply give abstract throughts about witnessing. Rather, as an exile on Patmos "on account of the word of God and the testimony of Jesus" (1:9), he wrote as a pastor in a setting of persecution and encouraged faithful witness by all his readers. John's advice merits a new hearing. Numerous obstacles confront the gospel of Christ today. Quality evangelism is a must if regenerate churches are to thrive in an environment of competing theologies, philosophies, and ideologies.

Evangelism by all members of Baptist churches has been a recurring theme in covenants prepared by many different Baptist groups. The 1853 covenant of J. Newton Brown, which has had wide circulation among both American and Southern Baptists, includes the pledge "to seek the salvation of our kindred and acquaintances."[6] A model covenant of the Free Will Baptists contains the vow that church members will "commend [their] religion to others" and "spread Christian knowledge and diffuse the Christian spirit in society and among all the nations of the earth."[7] To "be instrumental in bringing men to a saving knowledge of our Lord and Saviour, Jesus Christ" is a basic commitment of those affirming a model Seventh Day Baptist covenant.[8] In a covenant used by the General Baptists, church members agree to cooperate "in every enterprise having for its end the glory of God and the salvation of men."[9] Thus, the covenantal precedents of Baptists measure up to New Testament teaching that sharing the good news of Christ belongs to all Christians.

What are some practical ways to help church members recognize and respond to the evangelistic imperative which is central to the life of the church? First, a church's evangelism committee can sponsor a widely advertised, well-prepared three-night evangelism conference. Rather than be a time simply to hear evangelistic sermons, the conference will focus on a serious study of issues relating to local church witnessing. The first night can concentrate on foundations for witness by the total membership as expressed in the New Testament and demonstrated in Baptist history. The second night can face squarely reasons for reluctance to evangelize and discuss creative alternatives. Testimonies by those experienced in sharing their faith can then be the focal point of the third night. To be successful, such a conference will need strong leadership and wide participation by members.

Second, a church staff can make a comprehensive list of those members who are known to be effective in sharing their witness with non-Christians. The staff can then hold a meeting with these people. The goal of the meeting is to encourage accomplished witnesses to cultivate the evangelistic potential of other members of the congregation. Each person attending the meeting can be guided to do two things: to call or visit another member and explore his or her interest in doing personal evangelism and to form a visitation team with that person for several weeks or months. After sufficient time has elapsed, members who have been trained in evangelism through this process and have had exciting witnessing experiences should be given an opportunity to share before the church some of the values and joys personal witnessing has for them.

BUILD INFORMED EVANGELISM

When Jesus encountered a woman of Samaria who came to draw water from a well (John 4), he talked with her about the water of eternal life and helped her see herself in proper perspective. Jesus identified himself as the Messiah expected by the woman. Astounded by this news she responded immediately by hurrying into the city of Sychar and telling its people about "a man who told me all that I ever did" (4:29). The result was that "many Samaritans from that city believed in him because of the woman's testimony" (4:39). An obvious lesson to be learned from this account is that it is perfectly in order for us to share good news about Jesus with others as soon as we hear and experience it. Further, the results of such spontaneous witnessing can be amazing!

New Testament evangelism has another side, however. This side says that evangelism can sometimes be more effective when it is more fully informed. Early in his ministry Jesus called Simon and Andrew to be "fishers of men." Other disciples received similar claims on their lives. The call of these men to be witnesses was followed by years of education by the Teacher. For Jesus, evangelism and instruction were essential complements. Jesus trained witnesses by example, by teaching, by preaching. The life, death, and resurrection of Jesus, the commission of Matthew 28:18-20 and Acts 1:8, and the standards for evangelistic work established in the revival of Pentecost (Acts 2) comprised the basic instructional foundation for the evangelistic fervor of the early church.

Just as a theological seminary teaches students those subjects which make evangelism more effective, as well as offers devotional experiences leading to spiritual preparation for evangelism and other ministries, a church should do the same for its members. A church does well to be cautious about placing heavy evangelistic demands on new members before adequately preparing them for witnessing responsibilities. What are key areas of evangelistic instruction for all members of Baptist churches? Certainly the following can be included:

1. *Knowledge of the Holy Spirit.* Acts 1:8 clearly shows that witnessing must be preceded by a powerful experience with the Holy Spirit in the life of each Christian. Church members need to be keenly attuned to the continuing work of the Holy Spirit in every phase of their spiritual growth. A church can facilitate such an awareness through corporate worship and the sponsorship of personal and family worship. Evangelism cannot exist unless the Holy Spirit is recognized as its driving force. Knowing the Holy Spirit is a primary credential for anyone desiring to share a Christian testimony.

2. *Knowledge of the Bible.* Encounters with non-Christians will necessitate a solid understanding of biblical truth. A Christian witness cannot present his or her case without this understanding. The objections and reasons raised by the evangelized for not becoming Christian can put considerable stress on any Christian who delivers a biblically illiterate witness. Bible training can come through regular Sunday church school programs, but special

courses in the biblical area should at least be made available by the church staff for those members who are earnestly trying to do evangelistic work.

3. *Information about the history of evangelism.*[10] A look at past evangelistic efforts and trends will alert witnesses in local churches to the strengths and weaknesses which have characterized evangelism in Christian history. This kind of study can help contemporary witnesses discover ways to accomplish evangelism effectively, understand the significant witnessing achievements of their Christian predecessors, and create a historical identification with the people of God in the ministry of evangelism. The church history committee and the church evangelism committee can work in conjunction with the church staff to design and implement such a study.

4. *Familiarity with skills of communication and interpersonal relations.* Church witnesses need to know the fine distinction between compassionate persuasion and subtle manipulation. They need to be able to talk comfortably with non-Christians and to share their faith with ease and confidence. Opportunities should be arranged for church witnesses to sit through several sessions with a minister who is trained in clinical pastoral education. An improved knowledge of self, an increased appreciation for interpersonal relations, and a new understanding of how to communicate one's self and one's message are important elements which can be learned through such sessions and will contribute to more efficient evangelistic work.

5. *Knowledge of Baptist history and of the programs of the church represented by the witness.*[11]Although the goal of evangelism is to bring persons to the salvation of Jesus Christ, persons who receive Christ at the invitation of church witnesses are likely to be inquisitive about the denominations and churches of these witnesses. Thus, the witnesses should possess basic facts about Baptist history, about the doctrines and practices of Baptists, and about the opportunities which their churches can offer new Christians. A brochure describing church programs should be available for witnesses to share with people whom they visit.

6. *Some grasp of the potential results of personal evangelism.* Church members who have succeeded in evangelism can give testimonies that will make witnessing all the more appealing to new witnesses. Knowledge that just one person has discovered

God's redemption and experienced a changed life is all the reward necessary for one's efforts. But the result can be even greater than that, for the new convert may accomplish great things for God. For example, someone shared the good news with Martin Luther King, Jr.; and someone shared it with Billy Graham. The witnesses behind the scene likely had little thought that these new Christians would eventually exert such tremendous Christian influence on the world.

A story told in 1925 by M. E. Dodd, pastor of the First Baptist Church of Shreveport, Louisiana, vividly illustrates the preceding point. Two men lived in the same city. One lived a wicked life and spent his money on corrupting forms of recreation. The other, a Christian philanthropist, used his money to build churches, orphanages, hospitals, and schools. Dodd continued:

> Just a little while ago an old Baptist preacher . . . passed away. . . . He died in borrowed clothes and on a bed that was not his own. This was the preacher who baptized that great philanthropist, when he was but a barefoot boy out in the country. And I have an idea that when the Great and Righteous Judge of all the earth calls this great servant of his up for his reward that he will also call for the old preacher, and ask him to stand by the great man's side, and to receive an equal reward.[12]

7. *Knowledge that healthy evangelism includes education.* The "dip them and drop them" aspersion has sometimes been cast on Baptists for their alleged strong attention to initial conversion experiences and baptismal statistics and their inadequate efforts to inform the recently evangelized and baptized of their covenantal obligations. Evangelism and Christian education are kinsmen.

> A strong and defensible program of evangelism . . . does not aim at a single initial decision and no more. It rather strives for a continuing renewal of personal commitment to God in Christ, a development of God-given talents and opportunities for his service, an interpretation of every relationship and responsibility of life in the light of the Christian faith, and a lifelong growth in Christian maturity. The full and final intention of evangelism requires, for its achievement, the work of teaching and training.[13]

A church must realize that its entire program is somehow related to evangelism. This includes Sunday church school, Christian training classes, music programs, and other ministries. Evangelism is not simply one segment of a church's life; it is a permeating concern of a church's total life. Christian education is an essential feature of wholesome evangelism.

LEGITIMATE EVANGELISM CAN TAKE MANY SHAPES

Jesus Christ frequently chose to share the good news of God's revelation in eyeball to eyeball encounters with individuals. His meeting with Zacchaeus (Luke 19) plainly showed his approach to personal evangelism. First, he recognized a thin shell of a man who was searching, although timidly, for new meaning in his life. Second, Jesus exercised initiative and invited himself into the home of Zacchaeus where the two could doubtlessly talk in private about the deepest concerns and needs of Zacchaeus's life. Third, after sensing the repentant spirit of Zacchaeus, Jesus announced, "Today salvation has come to this house" (19:9).

Jesus also shared the good news of God with masses of people at one time. The Sermon on the Mount and the feeding of the five thousand are cases in point. Through parables, miracles, helping ministries, and personal obedience to his Father in heaven, Jesus regularly communicated truth and self to throngs of people. One gets the impression from observing how Jesus dealt with groups of people that his message was not directed to nebulous, unidentifiable masses of humanity but to individuals within the groups.

The shape of Jesus' approach to sharing the good news of God's special revelation was diversified. Baptists have successfully adapted the principle of diversification into their own witnessing patterns. Camp meetings, revivals, evangelistic crusades, lay evangelism, visitation evangelism, educational evangelism, courses on evangelism in seminary curricula, divisions of evangelism in major mission boards, evangelism through social ministries, and the use of such media as radio, television, and puppets are just some of the evangelistic forms which Baptists have employed.

Baptists were among the primary benefactors of the Great Awakening of the 1730s and 1740s. Out of the Awakening grew a tremendous surge of evangelism, particularly among the prorevivalist Separate Baptists who emerged from New England Congregationalism. With a strong emphasis on a vital personal faith prior to baptism, the Separate Baptists contributed significantly to the growth of Baptist life in New England. They made their greatest impact in the South, however. Shubal Stearns and Daniel Marshall became Separate Baptists in New England. "Their coming to Virginia and North Carolina marked the beginning of . . . far-reaching evangelism among the Baptists."[14]

To be sure, it is virtually impossible to understand the evangelistic fervor of the Southern Baptist Convention without some knowledge of the influence of the Separate Baptists. The first Separate Baptist church in the South was at Sandy Creek, North Carolina. Founded in 1755 with Shubal Stearns as its pastor, this church became the center from which emanated some of the most remarkable evangelistic achievements recorded in Baptist history! The church "began with 16 souls; and in a short-time increased to 606."[15] Further, within seventeen years it became the "mother, grandmother, and great grandmother to 42 churches, from which sprang 125 ministers."[16] The Sandy Creek Baptist Association was formed in 1758 as the third Baptist association in America.

Separate Baptist evangelism took many shapes. Lay Christians witnessed to their neighbors on farms. Pastors delivered sermons which reflected a warm message of conversion. Churches sent out itinerant evangelists to bear witness to Christ in areas without churches. The association meetings were used to share evangelistic appeals with non-Christian participants. The camp meeting was an especially useful evangelistic tool. Samuell Harriss was an effective itinerant Separate Baptist evangelist in Virginia, and hundreds of people regularly traveled many miles and camped at the places of his meetings to attend services for several days. Harriss and a colleague once baptized seventy-five persons at one time, and on one of their journeys, which lasted several weeks, they baptized more than two hundred.[17]

In view of the multiple shapes of evangelism exhibited in our own Baptist heritage, and in view of the various approaches Jesus took in sharing the gospel expressed in his own person, how can we adapt the principle of diversification into contemporary programs of Christian witnessing which both manifest and stimulate a regenerate church membership? Two basic points need to be made.

First, individual church members should feel free to share in those shapes of evangelism with which they are most comfortable and through which they can make the best contributions. A church does well to place before its members on a continuing basis a firm biblical, historical, and theological foundation for doing evangelism. Motivation must precede shape. Then the church staff, the church evangelism committee, and church training classes are in a position to offer members specific and practical frameworks within which they can do the witnessing work of the church—such as team visitation witnessing on a designated night of the week or a prison ministry on Sunday morning. Some members will not do witnessing unless they are given concrete guidelines by the church. A church serves these members best by clearly outlining some evangelistic shapes for them.

On the other hand, some church members are so creative and zealous that they develop individualized and unique styles of evangelism. (For example, when I was younger, a laundry truck driver who was Sunday School superintendent in my home church performed active evangelistic witness to people on his route every day. Evangelism for him was not an occasional unwanted duty; it was the joyful expression of the Spirit of God within him.) As long as the evangelistic patterns of these free-spirited members are not contradictory to the purposes and tasks of the church, they should be given full encouragement. A full measure of the priesthood of believers should be allowed in the accomplishment of evangelistic goals, and members who witness in their own way—rather than in the official Thursday night visitation program—should not be made to feel guilty. If evangelism to them is a life-style rather than a weekly or monthly assignment (it is almost humorous to think of Jesus bearing witness to his Father just one night a week), they may well be making the more important accomplishments anyway.

Sometimes members can hide behind certain shapes of evangelism to the neglect of others. Contributions to evangelism are made by the person monitoring the sound system, the usher who gives a warm greeting, the member who places money in an offering plate, the teacher in a church class, and so on. These contributions are imperative. In a sense, however, they are adjunct to the New Testament mandate that every Christian assume an active posture in doing evangelism in all phases of life. No ultimate substitutions can be made for person-to-person conversations with non-Christians. To do less is to miss the total potential inherent in personal witnessing.

Second, the shape of evangelism can and should vary from church to church. Bus evangelism may work well for one church, television evangelism for another, apartment evangelism for a third, resort evangelism for a fourth, and the list is endless. For this reason a church evangelism committee has a special responsibility to keep a close eye on the changing character of the church's community. Opportunities for ministry may have arisen quickly for which the church has formulated no evangelistic strategy. During the several-month period devoted to the writing of this book, within one-half mile of my house a major apartment complex has been completed; new condominiums have been constructed; and numerous houses have been finished. A church that does not perform regular community surveys will likely limit itself to evangelistic shapes which will not meet growing needs. Progressivism must be a constant feature of a church's witnessing outlook.

Baptist associations can play a mighty role in helping churches see the need for new evangelistic styles. Just as the Philadelphia Association sent John Gano to the South to meet evangelistic needs there in the middle of the eighteenth century, associations today can monitor community developments, alert churches to evangelistic possibilities, and provide resources to assist churches in meeting these needs. Associations are in an excellent position to help churches do what they ought in sharing the good news of Jesus Christ.

EVANGELIZE RESPECTFULLY, INTELLIGENTLY, AND EXPECTANTLY

Primary to bearing a Christian witness is the need to realize that all persons receiving the witness are made in the image of God. Thus, they are not to be treated as pawns to be shoved around or as nails to be pounded. Instead, they are to be related to with a deep concern for their spiritual well-being that respects their individuality, honors their intelligence, and hopes for their conversion. Evangelism cannot be applied like paint to a wall. A wall is inanimate and has no vote as to whether it will be coated. Evangelism involves the interaction of at least two human personalities plus that of the Holy Spirit. "As you wish that men would do to you, do so to them" (Luke 6:31) is an excellent rule to remember in sharing a witness.

The question of the rich young man, "Good Teacher, what must I do to inherit eternal life?" (Mark 10:17) made possible a special opportunity for Jesus to share the "good news" with the man. Jesus took the man seriously, and a healthy encounter ensued. Jesus did not dodge the question; he used the occasion to affirm the man's understanding of basic Old Testament commandments. Rather than be evasive, Jesus brought the man to terms with his fundamental failure—an inordinate love of money. The evangelistic appeal of Jesus was for the man to give his possessions to the poor and to follow Christ. The response could be conversion or rejection. The rich young man chose the latter.

The lessons of this account are important for contemporary witnesses. One, Jesus did not play games with this potential Christian. He dealt earnestly with the man's plea for understanding and treated him with dignity. Two, Jesus gave a direct answer to a direct question. He recognized what appeared to be a teachable moment and took full advantage of it. Three, Jesus used Scripture to affirm the man's awareness of essential features of the Old Testament Covenant, and then Jesus "looking upon him loved him" and presented him with the challenge to adopt the New Covenant of God in Christ. The man said "no" to the invitation and went away. Four, Jesus doubtlessly felt badly for the man when he rejected ultimate meaning for his life, but Jesus did not allow himself to be overtaken with a sense of personal failure because of the man's response. Jesus did what he could! Also, Jesus did not chase the man down and try to "beat some sense" into his head. Rather, Jesus redeemed the occasion by teaching his disciples a lesson about the difficulty those with riches have in entering the kingdom of heaven.

Curious evangelistic techniques have sometimes characterized the witnessing behavior of Baptists. Emotionalism reached such extremes among the Separate Baptists of the 1700s that it was fairly common "to have a large proportion of a congregation prostrate on the floor"; to hear "screams, cries, groans, songs, shouts, and hosannas, notes of grief and notes of joy, all heard at the same time, [which] made a heavenly confusion, a sort of undescribable concert," and at association meetings to find several ministers in different parts of the congregation at the same time either exhorting, praying, or arguing with opponents of the gospel.[18]

Such emotional excesses may seem alien to the sophistication of the twentieth-century Baptist mind-set. However, lest we isolate the Separate Baptists as the only Baptist group ever to have resorted to manipulative evangelism, we should take a hard look at the growing tendency among some Baptists today to baptize more and more preschoolers. This is a tragic trend which does violence to a cardinal distinctive of Baptists. Primary evangelistic attention can better be directed to young people and adults. Converted parents will take seriously the spiritual needs of their children. Converted preschoolers (an ironic combination of words) will have less chance of stimulating non-Christian parents to change weak moral and spiritual habits. Evangelistic fortitude is the issue at stake. Even if it requires more preparation, inner strength, and positive determination to witness face to face with an adult than with a preschooler, we must give priority to the former option. Manipulative evangelism may achieve the fastest results, but the long-term positive effects are likely to be rather poor. Evangelism with integrity in intention and implementation will lead to a desirable victory, for one will know that one has done all that is possible.

When a salesman at my door lets loose all the stops in his effort to sell me his product, red caution flags appear before my eyes. When a member of a para-church religious body apprehends me in an airport terminal, pins a carnation to my jacket before I know what has happened, and solicits money for a non-Christian religious cause, I become resentful. Whenever someone tries to con me into doing anything, I question the validity of the enterprise.

Non-Christians are persons who have some sense of self-respect and some measure of intelligence. Although they have not responded favorably to God, they are still part of God's creation. God loves them. God has compassion for them. God works through Christians to share the good news of Christ with them. We are not to thrust ourselves upon strangers like vampires in the night. Rather, we must earn their respect; we must develop avenues of communication; and sometimes only then can we begin to talk with someone about the deepest and most intimate phases of his or her life. We must cultivate friendships which open doors for creative discussion of spiritual affairs. The doors may not swing as fast as we would like, but it is better to gain a slow and responsible entrance into someone's life than to rush in like a wild animal. For Jesus, respect for human personality was more important than evangelistic statistics.

A church evangelism committee will do well to offer church members a workshop dealing with evangelistic procedures. A look at how Jesus approached evangelism will be particularly useful. Suggestions by veteran witnesses are a conspicuous resource for such a workshop. In simulated witnessing experiences, trainees can knock on doors and meet various kinds of people who have different responses to the appeals of the witnesses. These responses should reflect statements of anticipated opposition. Following each simulated experience, all persons present can share thoughts about the ways the evangelistic encounter might be handled better. The ultimate goal of such a workshop is to send out new church witnesses who feel so comfortable with procedures and techniques that they are able to give basic attention to the persons to whom they minister. Person-centered and God-oriented evangelism is the true objective.

Pastors, better than anyone else, can set the pattern for an evangelistic ministry that respects persons and their needs. A pastor genuinely concerned about sharing Christ and spiritual values with non-Christians will be a model evangelist for the church membership. The pastor will inject witnessing stamina into the regenerate quality of the church. He or she will give his or her congregation a reason to witness, techniques for doing it, resources for making it successful, and a word of appreciation for accepting the privilege. The church motivated by the Holy Spirit will then set out to make the Great Commission more than a motto. Evangelism will become a life-style.

Church Membership in Service

To this point we have concentrated largely on regenerate church membership in terms of either individual members or entire congregations. The regenerate qualities of a church also are closely related to the quality of life of small groups within the church. Much of the Christian service rendered by churches occurs through small group ministries. Small groups constantly facilitate quality growth in the spiritual life of churches. "Reflection upon church history makes evident the fact that small committed, disciplined groups of Christians have often been instruments of religious and moral renewal. . . ."[1] Further, Elton Trueblood, an astute observer of American church life for several decades, has pointed out that churches will become increasingly aware of the power of their small groups.[2]

Biblical precedents for small group work are plentiful. Luke recorded in Acts 6:1-6 that seven men were chosen to assist in ministering to the needs of widows. Further, the twelve disciples selected by Jesus were a small group assigned to exemplify and make known the things God was accomplishing through his obedient Son. Both of these groups were to operate within the purposes of God for the Christian community.

97

Baptist churches carry out a whole host of their functions through small groups. Bible teaching takes place in Sunday School classes. Discipleship development occurs in church training groups. Christian witnessing receives attention among visitation teams. Community service results from the work of deacon bodies. Church planning and business assume priority in the church council and in various committees. Church administration is accomplished through church staffs. Music ministries prosper in graded choir programs. Thus, in one sense a Baptist church is a composite community of small groups.

SMALL GROUPS AND REGENERATE CHURCH MEMBERSHIP

How are small groups related to a regenerate church membership? Perhaps one way to answer this is to pose some hypothetical situations which show obvious ways that small groups can exhibit nonregenerate features. If a church staff opposes key ingredients in the biblical mission of the church, then the staff's approach to leadership will not help those ministries which offer the regeneration of the Holy Spirit to non-Christians and which encourage a high level of moral and spiritual integrity among those who have already experienced "rebirth." If a deacon body functions exclusively in the areas of church business, administration, and management to the neglect of the more caring, supportive, and service-oriented kinds of ministries, such as visitation, charity, and teaching, then it is doubtful that the deacon body is fulfilling the biblical expectations of regenerate deacons. If a nominating committee chooses candidates on the bases of nepotism, personality, and wealth, with little genuine consideration for spiritual qualifications, then the committee makes recommendations which are less than regenerate in motivation. If a Sunday School class, instead of engaging in serious exploration of the content of the Bible and its importance for daily living, spends most of its time in small talk and gossip and is bored with a teacher who is unprepared, then the class and the teacher are doing little to meet the regenerate possibilities which can grow out of solid Bible study.

On the other hand, small groups can exert a monumental impact on the nature of a regenerate church membership when they do their work well and enthusiastically under God's guidance.

The exciting fact is that church staffs, deacon bodies, committees, classes, and other small groups in churches have the potential to raise the regenerate life-style and goals of congregations to unbelievable heights. Just like the twelve disciples, small groups in Baptist churches sometimes have weaknesses and occasionally individuals in the groups deviate from spiritual objectives. But let it never be forgotten that the faith and commitment of the early disciples had an inestimable influence on the rise of the Christian church in the face of countless odds. Small groups in churches today can also have positive influence far out of proportion to their size. When this occurs, the regenerate nature of churches rises with affirmative momentum toward the biblical ideal.

The church renewal movement in American Christianity has both stressed the importance of small groups in church life and demonstrated their ability to enhance the regenerate integrity of church membership. Particular attention in renewal writings has been given to the formation and use of covenants by church groups.[3] These covenants comprise the disciplines to which group members commit themselves and upon which they construct meaningful work and ministry. Such covenants must be rooted deeply in Scripture. A goal of this chapter is to suggest additional disciplines and principles upon which church groups can mature and serve Christ.

In the course of writing this chapter, I have been the beneficiary of the graciousness of many small groups in my own church (Judson Baptist Church) in Nashville, Tennessee. Soon after I began the chapter, my wife (Mary Jane) suffered a miscarriage complicated by low blood pressure (sinking at one point to thirty over zero), by peritonitis, and by septic shock. This resulted in exploratory abdominal surgery, three days and nights in an intensive care unit, and a hospital stay of eleven days. She is recovering remarkably well as I write, though she was in critical condition only a few days ago and made an unexpected visit "through the valley of the shadow of death."

How did small groups in Judson Church respond? Our Sunday School class sent cards and food. Members of the class made telephone contacts and visited the hospital. Our church training class sent flowers. A representative of the deacons visited our home. The entire church staff reflected an interest, and the pastor (Raymond Langlois) ministered long and compassionately. All of these groups indicated that they had special prayer in Mary Jane's behalf. Small groups in at least three other churches also told me of special prayers they had. These groups sent cards, flowers, and food, as well, and made personal contacts. God worked a healing miracle with Mary Jane, and the intercessory concern of small groups in Baptist churches was a real factor in the healing process. My appreciation for small groups in Baptist' church life has reached a level never before experienced—and just in time to express even more deeply my belief that these groups can add immeasurably to the regenerate ministries which only a New Testament congregation can offer.

The presupposition behind the following pages is that small groups in churches exist to serve. True, Sunday School classes study the Bible; church training groups discuss applications of their faith; committees perform business; and staffs administrate. Ultimately, group meetings are for naught if they do not result in Christian service to God, other Christians, and the nonchurched. Individuals in churches can and do engage in all sorts of meaningful ministries, but the collective ministries done by groups can often result in more effective and comprehensive service to a total community.

Since many kinds of groups are constantly at work in Baptist churches, no attempt will be made to deal with all of them. Space is prohibitive. Instead, attention will focus primarily on one group—deacons. The New Testament ideal is that deacons are to be model church servants. The Greek word *diakonos* can be translated "deacon" or "servant." Servanthood is explicit in the diaconal position. The principles for effective diaconal work which are enunciated in this chapter have immediate ramifications for most other small groups in Baptist churches. Ways to apply each principle to these groups will be described.

ROOTED IN SCRIPTURE

Models for Christian service through deacon bodies exist plainly in the New Testament. Prototypes of deacons appear in Acts 6:1-6. More direct references to deacons are in Philippians 1:1 and 1 Timothy 3:8-13. Two significant points emerge from a careful evaluation of the New Testament evidence concerning deacons. First, biblical qualifications for deacons are high. Deacons are expected to have exemplary Christian lives. The promise of 1 Timothy 3:13 is for deacons who serve well: "Those who serve well as deacons gain a good standing for themselves and also great confidence in the faith which is in Christ Jesus." Deacons who claim this promise by carefully heeding biblical qualifications for their office can render compassionate ministries worthy of imitation by other church members.

Second, deacons are servants of God and the church and are therefore vital to the nature and being of the church. The New Testament "affords unambiguous evidence of the perpetual necessity of *diakonia* [service] as a function of the Church on earth."[4] The early church crystallized the work of *diakonia* in the office of deacon. Deacons had more than peripheral value to the church. Because of the apparent lack of exact prototypes for deacons in Jewish or other sources, deacons probably arose in the New Testament period to meet the urgent need for special church servants.[5] Deacons are crucial to fulfilling the service tasks of Baptist churches as well.

For deacons and other small groups in churches what can be learned from this history? To begin with, no small group has a right to exist unless its reason for being has a foundation in the Bible. Although it is not essential, for example, to locate a direct reference to a nominating committee in the New Testament, it is of paramount importance to recognize that Jesus himself carefully selected and trained Christian leaders (such as the twelve disciples) and that he took this privilege seriously, for the whole future of the church was at stake in the newly chosen leadership.

Also, every small group in church life should possess strong biblical qualifications for its participants. One way to accomplish this is to write out the qualifications in a group covenant (see Appendix D for an example). This document can be useful in orienting new group members and in reminding present members of their continuing commitments.

Further, every church group exists to serve, or else it misinterprets its reason for being. A Sunday School class is not just for Bible study and fellowship, as important as they are. Bible study is a prelude to ministry. A church choir is justified in improving its sound, its look, and its quality through excellent training, superior accompaniment, and beautiful robes, but the choir does not complete its task until it serves God and the church through musical worship and careful cultivation of an environment in which God's Spirit can speak to and be heard by the congregation.

Any small group in a Baptist church which cannot find a basis for its existence in the Bible, or which does not possess high biblical standards for its members, or which does not exist to serve has outlived its usefulness. Evaluation of such a group should lead either to its termination or to a structuring around the common purpose and mission of the church. Creative groups tied closely to biblical intentions must be the order of the day if regenerate church practices are to achieve full reality. Incidentally, every small group will find it a healthy adventure to read the Bible in group meetings and isolate those passages which seem particularly appropriate for its work.

BALANCED IN MEMBERSHIP

Deacon bodies need to be comprised of church members representing various age groups and levels of experience. Another factor which many Baptist churches consider important is a balance between male and female deacons. To illustrate a historical pattern of which numerous Baptists are not aware, women deacons (or deaconesses) have been a part of Baptist life since the 1600s. Thomas Helwys, who became the pastor of the first Baptist church in England about 1611, claimed that deaconesses, along with other church officers, were to be elected and approved by their church with fasting, prayer, and the laying on of hands.[6] The Broadmead Baptist Church in Bristol, England, chose a deaconess in 1662, another in 1673, and three others in 1679.[7]

Morgan Edwards, earliest historian of Baptists in America, made references to deaconesses in several writings between 1770 and 1774. For example, he mentioned deaconesses in nine Separate Baptist churches in Virginia,[8] three in North Carolina,[9] and one in South Carolina.[10] Edwards favored deaconesses and cited Romans 16:1 and 1 Timothy 3:11 as biblical bases for them.[11]

Five conclusions can be drawn from a more complete look at the role of women deacons in our Baptist past:[12]

(1) Although deaconesses have existed in every century of Baptist life, the position has never been widespread.

(2) Likely reasons why deaconesses have been few in number include the brevity of biblical information on them, varying views of the biblical data which does exist, a strong identification of the diaconate with church management coupled with the American

proclivity to keep participation of women in management positions at a minimal level, general sociological and cultural biases against women which have manifested themselves in church life, and the contentment of churches to let men do diaconal work and the consequent absence of any reason to raise the deaconess issue.

(3) Two of the more flourishing periods for deaconesses have been the latter 1700s and the present. Basic thrusts toward liberation in American life lay behind and within both of these periods.

(4) Deaconesses seem to have flourished best in those times when the diaconate has been interpreted more in terms of a wide range of supporting and caring ministries rather than more narrowly in terms of church management and business administration.

(5) Baptist churches with deaconesses have had various practices regarding them. Some churches have ordained deaconesses; others have not. Some churches have given female deacons equality of responsibilities with male deacons; others have not. Some churches have designated women in the diaconate as deaconesses; others as women deacons.

A church nominating committee should take an inventory of all small groups for which it has the responsibility to make recommendations to the church for new group members. The goal of the inventory is to uncover any imbalances in small group memberships. The nominating committee may discover that just as its deacon body is all men, other groups may unnecessarily be all women, or all youth, or all senior citizens, or all wealthy, or all inexperienced, or whatever. Careful attention to broadening the scope of a committee's membership may make for more productive work by the committee and will certainly improve the representation of the church's membership on the committee. As some churches have enhanced their ministries to women through women deacons, the churches may also find that other small groups with a more equitable balance of membership can lead to advancements in total church program effectiveness.

Some churches may want to give more serious consideration than ever before to having women in professional staff positions. Besides being enrolled in music ministry and religious education programs at Baptist seminaries, more and more women are working on degrees in theology, and more and more women are receiving ordination as ministers. In addition to the pastorate, reappraisal of congregational needs may reveal special areas of ministry where ordained women can serve more effectively than men. Each church will need to cope with this situation in its own way; but if Donald F. Thomas is correct, the important question for modern churches is "not whether women should hold positions in the church but whether the modern church can fulfill its ministry without them."[13]

ACCOUNTABLE TO CHURCH

Every small group in a church is answerable to the church for its spirit and actions. A group cannot responsibly work independently of the purpose and mission of the whole congregation. Deacon history shows plainly how Baptist churches have used ordination, discipline, trial periods for special training, and other measures to insert accountability into the structure of deacon bodies.

In the past, churches have variously included in ordination procedures for deacons an examination of the candidates, fasting, prayer, a sermon describing biblical qualifications, a charge from the minister, and the laying on of hands. Through ordination deacons have received authority from God, the Bible, and the local church. Ordination is given by the church to deacons to set them aside for special ministries and leadership roles. Ordination helps deacons know that their church has high expectations of them.

The other side of the coin is that, because of the covenantal agreement made with a church in ordination, deacons are subject to the discipline of the ordaining church if they violate their ordination. The constitution approved by the Baptist church in Amersham, England, in 1675 claimed that "if . . . deacons shall Asume Any power or prerogative Above ye Church . . . that thee Church shall Judg & the Lord by his word shall give they defined sentance."[14] In 1685 the First Baptist Church of Boston, Massachusetts, dismissed Edward Dinker from his work as a deacon for "neglecting to officiate in his place for a long time and persisting in soe doeing."[15]

Still another approach to insuring deacon accountability was reflected in a proposal adopted by the Baptist church in Fenstanton, England, in 1652. Recognizing the role of deacons in church finances, the church's proposal, which created an audit check, stated that "the deacons should give up their accounts every half-year, at the least; because our experience doth declare that some, denying their principles, have been excommunicated without giving up their accounts, to the loss of the congregation." [16]

All church groups will do well to learn the lesson of accountability to the church. One of the problems with the church renewal movement is that many dissatisfied church members have frequently attempted to reform their churches by forming search groups which are barely related to the churches. Rather than be a healthy leaven of transformation within their churches, these groups are sometimes alienated bodies of Christians who sit outside their churches and throw critical darts at the way things are going inside them. These groups need to search more deeply for the full content of Ephesians 4:16: "the whole body [of Christ], joined and knit together by every joint with which it is supplied, when each part is working properly, makes bodily growth and upbuilds itself in love." Only when a group accepts its accountable relationship with its church is it in a viable position to formulate responsible strategies for renewal and to design creative alternatives for current church programs.

Groups which respect their accountability to their church will work within the organizational and doctrinal framework of the church, will align themselves aggressively with the goals of the church, and will execute their responsibilities with an eagerness to magnify God and the church, rather than selfish ambitions. Perhaps the church staff can meet periodically with all small group leaders so that together they can make common decisions about the spiritual direction of the church and the role of the groups in forming this direction.

The church council may find it helpful to do a study of presently existing groups to determine whether gaps of accountability exist with any of them. If the answer is yes, the council may want to suggest to such a group ways that it can improve its relationship with the total thrust of the church. New groups which come into being should be alerted at the outset by the church staff to the nature and mission of the church.

DIVERSE IN FUNCTIONS

Each small group in a Baptist church has a variety of duties to fulfill. Therefore, it is important for each group to create a comprehensive set of assignments for its members which assures that all the jobs get done and that the most urgent jobs get done first. For a group to focus all its attention on a single role is to neglect a broader range of possible ministries. If deacons, for example, did nothing but distribute the Lord's Supper, they would make a mockery of the wealth of service opportunities which are theirs. The fact is, however, that Baptist history is saturated with vivid demonstrations of diaconal involvement in a wide range of ministries.

Prior to the beginnings of Baptist history, the Christian literature of the second through the fourth centuries showed that deacons functioned usefully in at least four broad areas. First, they were agents of charity. They visited the sick and imprisoned martyrs, provided clothing and burial for the dead, sought to restore excommunicated Christians, and cared for widows and orphans. Second, deacons were administrators. They kept order in worship, prepared utensils for the Lord's Supper, represented bishops at general councils, handled the church fund, and served generally as bishops' assistants in other matters. Third, deacons were teachers. They preached and trained new converts in catechetical classes. Last, deacons were worship leaders. They occasionally performed baptisms and regularly assisted in the Lord's Supper, including carrying bread and wine to those Christians absent from the Supper. Deacons also prayed and read Scripture in public worship.[17]

Deacons in Baptist history have also worked effectively in several areas of ministry. Many Baptist writings in the eighteenth and nineteenth centuries described diaconal work as consisting of service to three tables. First was the Lord's table, which involved providing and distributing the elements of the Lord's Supper to church members. Second was the table of the poor, which focused on ministry to the financially distressed and encouragement of church members to contribute money for benevolent purposes. Third was the table of the minister, which included inspection of a minister's needs and a prompting of church members to care for his necessities and comforts.

Unfortunately, a negative pattern began to develop among Baptist deacons in the early nineteenth century and is still very much a part of Baptist life today. This was the tendency to narrow the scope of diaconal work. Diaconal functions began to be viewed more and more in administrative, business, and management categories to the neglect of the more caring and supporting ministries. Baptist deacons were described as "the chief managers of the church" as early as 1773,[18] as "trustees of the church" as early as 1804,[19] and as a "board" as early as 1846.[20] As recently as 1958, an important article relating to the diaconate in Southern Baptist churches claimed that "the deacon usually renders an administrative and officiating ministry."[21] All this is not to suggest that all deacons operate exclusively as church business managers. Such is not the case, for hundreds of deacons are engaged, for example, in highly creative family ministry plans. The point is that there has been a major thrust over the past century toward a narrowing of diaconal work to one dominant area—administration. Fortunately, many healthy signs suggest that this thrust is gradually abating.

What is the relevance of this to other small groups in Baptist churches? Groups do well to recognize the actual breadth of their obligations, rather than simplistically to reduce their work to single tasks. Some may think, to illustrate, that all a nominating committee needs to do is nominate, or all a Sunday School class needs to do is spend one hour a week in Bible study. Far from it! A nominating committee needs to survey church membership talent, carefully evaluate the moral and spiritual credentials of possible church leaders, determine whether there are any age, sex, experience, or other imbalances in the makeup of existing small groups (a point discussed in detail earlier in this chapter), develop a sensitive appreciation for the importance of the church positions which are to be filled, approach prospective leaders about their willingness to assume certain positions if elected, meet over long periods of time, and engage in much prayer. Only then does the work of nomination come into play. A Sunday School must make adequate preparation for its meeting, study the Bible, engage in personal visitation to enlarge its membership, implement in life the practical implications of Bible study, enjoy social activities, and seek helpful ways to serve the community.

Think through the small groups with which you are related. Next, perform the simple exercise of listing the areas in which your groups actually function. Then list the areas in which you think your groups either can or should work. Are there any discrepancies in priorities between the two lists, and should some resolution be sought? If so, bring these to the attention of the groups. Suggest that all group members follow the same procedure. At a later time perhaps the members of each group can bring their evaluative thoughts together and map out improved strategies for accomplishing the tasks of the groups.

COMMITTED TO SERVICE

The primary reason for the existence of every small group in a Baptist church is to serve God and the church and thereby to assist the ministries of the church to its community and the world at large. If small group members are bent only on achieving private interests, they are depriving themselves of the chance to help a lot of people.

The Christian service afforded by small groups can take many forms. Deacon history vividly shows this. The prototypes for deacons in Acts 6 were selected to minister to widows. Church history demonstrates not only that deacon bodies have served but also that they have frequently done so in a most sacrificial manner. Three excellent examples will reveal the serving spirit of diaconal groups in action.

First, Bishop Dionysius of Alexandria described the charitable work of some deacons who ministered in a plague that befell Alexandria about A.D. 259: "They held fast to each other and visited the sick fearlessly, and ministered to them continually, serving them in Christ. And they died with them most joyfully, taking the affliction of others, and drawing the sickness from their neighbors to themselves and willingly receiving their pains." [22]

Second, near the end of the eighteenth century Sampson Bryan was a deacon in a Negro Baptist church in Savannah, Georgia. His brother, Andrew, was pastor.

> With his brother he [Sampson] was imprisoned and, like him, whipped until his back was torn and his blood puddled by his side on the ground in the sight of his vile persecutors. But he would not deny the Jesus whom he loved, nor consent to cease speaking His goodness. He shared with his brother the bitter persecution that the church was called upon to suffer in those days. Though missles [sic] most terrible from the enemy's camp were hurled against the church, this good man never faltered. He "purchased to himself a good degree and great boldness in the faith." He was much beloved by the church. He served the church faithfully until he fell asleep in Jesus early in the nineteenth century. [23]

Third, one writer showed how one deacon body went beyond its responsibilities in administration and in the Lord's Supper to a rather full involvement in social ministries. Writing in 1915, he spoke of

> the Judson Memorial Church . . . in lower New York, with its drinking fountain of ice-water at the corner, where thousands of the poor drink daily, its free dispensary for the help of the sick, its boarding-house for young men, its fresh-air home in the country, its many other lines of practical helpfulness; here the office of deacon is no figurehead affair. It stands for downright work. The passing of the cup is but an incident of solid weeks of ministration over a wide range of need.[24]

Whether it is a deacon body, a committee, a Bible study class, a church staff, a church council, trustees, or whatever, a small group needs to undergird all its work with various forms of compassionate Christian service. The regenerate character of church membership is at stake. Regenerate features of church life do not become fully realized when a group confines its work to meeting, talking, and socializing. Each small group has those things it normally does—administrate, study, nominate, usher, and others. The completion of these and similar tasks is fundamental to the success of a church. But a church must reach beyond those functions which keep its internal operations intact. Missions and ministries to a world in despair are imperative thrusts for a church which really cares about accepting the challenges of the New Testament. The appeal being made is for a more thorough and sacrificial investment of time by small groups in meeting these challenges. No group is exempt!

Appendix A
Church Covenant of
J. Newton Brown
(1853)

Source: *A New Baptist Church Manual,* **Revised (Valley Forge: Judson Press, 1976), pp. 9-11.**

Having been led, as we believe, by the Spirit of God to receive the Lord Jesus Christ as our Savior; and, on the profession of our faith, having been baptized in the name of the Father, and of the Son, and of the Holy Ghost, we do now, in the presence of God, angels, and this assembly, most solemnly and joyfully enter into covenant with one another, as one body in Christ.

We engage, therefore, by the aid of the Holy Spirit, to walk together in Christian love; to strive for the advancement of this church, in knowledge, holiness, and comfort; to promote its prosperity and spirituality; to sustain its worship, ordinances, discipline, and doctrines; to contribute cheerfully and regularly to the support of the ministry, the expenses of the church, the relief of the poor, and the spread of the gospel through all nations.

We also engage to maintain family and secret devotion; to educate our children religiously; to seek the salvation of our kindred and acquaintances; to walk circumspectly in the world; to be just in our dealings, faithful in our engagements, and exemplary in our deportment; to avoid all tattling, backbiting, and

111

excessive anger; to abstain from the sale and use of intoxicating drinks as a beverage; and to be zealous in our efforts to advance the kingdom of our Savior.

We further engage to watch over one another in brotherly love; to remember each other in prayer; to aid each other in sickness and distress; to cultivate Christian sympathy in feeling and courtesy in speech; to be slow to take offense, but always ready for reconciliation and mindful of the rules of our Savior to secure it without delay.

We moreover engage, that when we remove from this place, we will as soon as possible unite with some other church where we can carry out the spirit of this covenant and the principles of God's word.

Appendix B
Covenant of The Baptist Church of the Covenant (1972), Birmingham, Alabama

Source: *Baptist History and Heritage,* January, 1974, cover page 1.

I covenant before God, with this pastor, and congregation to do the following:

1. I will be faithful in attendance in worship and training.

2. I covenant to involve myself in at least one major ministry of the church.

3. I covenant to give of my means sacrificially, with the tithe as the basic guideline.

4. I covenant to live ethically and morally so that the cause of Christ is not weakened and the church shamed.

I am committed to an interracial, intercultural, and international church. I am committed to an innovative church—one that is warmly evangelical and socially concerned. I will strive mightily to assist the church to be a faithful people of God.

Appendix C
An Order of Service for Baptismal Worship Centering in a Church Covenant

Prelude: "Brethren, We Have Met to Worship"   Organist
Choral Prayer: "Take My Life and Let It Be"
Invocation: "Lord of the church, you who have given us the key to new life, keep us aware of the need to search out non-Christians, to teach them the good news of your salvation, and to baptize them in the name of the Father, the Son, and the Holy Spirit. Father, several new disciples choose to join your purposes and your church through believer's baptism. May they know the sacrifice of your Son which filled baptism with meaning, and may their obedience to you be full and complete. Let each feel a confirmation of his commitment and acceptance by the church and by the Holy Spirit. Unite all the members of this church (new and old) into a bond of love. Thank you for this time of baptismal celebration. Amen."
Scripture Readings: Matthew 3:13-17; Romans 6:3-4
Hymn of Commitment: "O Jesus, I Have Promised"
Offertory: "Living for Jesus"   Organist
Statement of Meditation (Pastor comments on meaning and purpose of baptism.)
Questioning of Candidates (Pastor and/or deacons ask the

114

following questions to each candidate either on the pulpit platform or in the baptismal pool.)
1) "What has God done in your life to lead you to this point?"
2) "What does believer's baptism mean to you?"
3) "Why do you wish to become a member of this church?"
Testimonial Responses of Candidates (Each candidate is given a brief amount of time to answer all three questions.)
Baptismal Covenant (Several candidates are in baptismal pool together. Pastor puts the contents of the church's covenant in the form of questions to which the candidates collectively respond, "We do." An example follows.[1])
PASTOR: "Do you covenant with God to seek:
to develop personal relationships with him;
to see where he is at work in his world and to join him in his work;
to speak on his behalf and to hear his word when it is spoken;
to demonstrate his love and to be open to receive it?"
CANDIDATES: "We do."
PASTOR: "Do you covenant with one another to seek:
to explore the meaning of being the continuing incarnation of God;
to build Christian community, affirming the worth of all persons;
to nurture each person as he grows in wisdom, faith, and personal relationships;
to help each person to discern his gifts and to call him to exercise these gifts;
to minister to one another, being sensitive to individuals, families, and groups, responding to needs with appropriate Christian action;
to help one another celebrate all of life;
to provide Christian education for your children, affirming your commitment to them during their most formative years;
to provide opportunities for worship, study, fellowship, mission action, and ministry;
to give systematically from your personal financial

[1] The covenant used here as an example is the highly creative covenant of the Glendale Baptist Church in Nashville, Tennessee.

resources, giving sacrificially when such giving is needed; to be accountable to one another for living faithfully in this covenant relationship?"

CANDIDATES: "We do."

PASTOR *(Lifts hands as a sign for the congregation to stand and addresses the congregation.):* "Believing that the church as the body of Christ is the continuing incarnation of God, do you also make this covenant with God and one another?"

CONGREGATION: "We do."

PASTOR: "Do you promise to give moral and spiritual support to these servants of God who are about to be baptized and to receive them into the fellowship of this church with gladness?"

CONGREGATION: "We do."

PASTOR *(Requests that all present bow their heads for prayer.):* "Eternal Father, thank you for Jesus Christ our Savior, who died for our sins, was buried, and was raised on the third day. Graciously receive these new servants who are putting on the Lord Jesus Christ in the covenant of baptism. Keep them faithful to you, your causes, and this church. Encourage them and us to a new vision of mission and ministry. Fill these baptismal initiations into the Christian life with the presence of the Holy Spirit. Amen."

Administration of Baptism (Congregation remains standing.)

Hymn of Discipleship: "Onward, Christian Soldiers"

Benediction: "Now may the God of peace who brought again from the dead our Lord Jesus, the great Shepherd of the sheep, by the blood of the eternal covenant, equip you with everything good that you may do his will, working in you that which is pleasing in his sight, through Jesus Christ; to whom be glory for ever and ever. Amen."

Postlude: "Wherever He Leads I'll Go"

Appendix D

Sunday School Workers' Covenant (1976) Woodmont Baptist Church, Nashville, Tennessee

Believing that the privilege of guiding people in the Christian way of life is worthy of my best, I covenant as a worker in the Sunday School of Woodmont Baptist Church to:

Order my conduct in keeping with the principles of the New Testament, and seek the help of the Holy Spirit that I may be faithful and efficient in my work (Ephesians 4:1).

Be regular and punctual in attendance, and, in case of unavoidable absence, give notice thereof as far in advance as possible (1 Corinthians 4:2).

Make thorough preparation of the lesson and for my other duties each week (2 Timothy 2:15).

Use the Bible with my group on Sunday morning, or other meeting times, and help them to understand and love it (Psalm 119:16).

Contribute my tithe to my church's budget (Malachi 3:10).

Attend the regular planning meetings (Luke 14:28-30).

Visit prospects frequently and make a special effort to contact absentees each week (Acts 2:46).

Study one or more books from the New Church Study Course each year (Proverbs 15:28a).

Cooperate wholeheartedly in the plans and activities of the church and school (1 Corinthians 3:9).

Be loyal to the program of the church, striving to attend all worship services (Hebrews 10:25).

Make witnessing a major endeavor (Proverbs 11:30).

Seek to discover and meet the needs of those with whom I come into contact, especially fellow church members and prospects for my church (Galatians 6:2).

Pray regularly for the church, the Sunday School, the officers and teachers, and for the pupils and the homes from which they come (1 Thessalonians 5:17).

Apply the teachings of Christ in moral and social issues of my everyday life (James 1:22).

With the help of God, I will do my utmost to keep this covenant.

Signed _____ Date _____

Notes

Chapter 1

[1] Personal letter, office of the General Secretary of the American Baptist Churches in the U.S.A., September 29, 1975.

[2] "Handbook Issue," *The Quarterly Review*, vol. 35 (July, 1975), pp. 7, 30.

[3] "Handbook Issue," *The Quarterly Review*, vol. 37 (July, 1977), p. 76.

[4] *Ibid.*, p. 91.

[5] Norman H. Maring and Winthrop S. Hudson, *A Baptist Manual of Polity and Practice* (Valley Forge: Judson Press, 1963), p. 15.

[6] Robert G. Torbet, *A History of the Baptists*, rev. ed. (Valley Forge: Judson Press, 1963), p. 487.

[7] M. R. Gordon, "Regeneration," *The New Bible Dictionary* (Grand Rapids: Wm. B. Eerdmans Publishing Co., 1962), p. 1081.

[8] *Ibid.*

[9] William L. Lumpkin, *Baptist Confessions of Faith*, rev. ed. (Valley Forge: Judson Press, 1969), p. 119.

[10] *Ibid.*, pp. 165, 228, 285ff., 365, 396. These pages refer to three illustrative English Baptist confessions of faith and three confessions of Baptists in America. Although there is no page given for the Philadelphia Confession of 1742, the reader should recognize that the wording in this document was the same as in the Second London Confession of 1677.

[11] *Ibid.*, pp. 120, 167, 291, 366. These pages refer to three representative English

Baptist statements of faith and two confessions of Baptists in America. As in footnote 10, no page is given for the Philadelphia Confession. The reader can again assume its similarity to the Second London Confession.

[12] *Ibid.*, pp. 120-121, 291, 293. The references here are to the 1611 confession of Thomas Helwys, the Second London Confession, and the Philadelphia Confession.

[13] *Ibid.*, pp. 286, 365. The Second London Confession, the Philadelphia Confession, and the New Hampshire Confession of 1833 are the references cited.

[14] *Ibid.*, pp. 168, 268, 364. The confessions cited here are the London Confession of 1644, the Second London Confession, the Philadelphia Confession, and the New Hampshire Confession.

[15] *Ibid.*, pp. 397-398. The citation is to the 1963 Statement of Faith of the Southern Baptist Convention.

[16] T. B. Maston, "Trends to Watch," *Capital Baptist*, August 21, 1975, p. 3.

[17] Lumpkin, *op. cit.*, p. 398.

[18] *Ibid.*, p. 285.

[19] Maring and Hudson, *op. cit.*, p. 37.

Chapter 2

[1] Norman H. Maring and Winthrop S. Hudson, *A Baptist Manual of Polity and Practice* (Valley Forge: Judson Press, 1963), pp. 72-73.

[2] Theodor H. Gaster, trans. and ed., *The Dead Sea Scriptures* (Garden City, N.Y.: Doubleday & Company, Inc., 1956), p. 47.

[3] Charles W. Deweese's "The Origin, Development, and Use of Church Covenants in Baptist History" (unpublished Ph.D. dissertation, Southern Baptist Theological Seminary, 1973) is a thorough treatment of the history of church covenants among Baptists.

[4] James Leo Garrett, "Seeking a Regenerate Church Membership," *Southwestern Journal of Theology*, vol. 3, no. 2 (April, 1961), p. 32.

[5] J. Herbert Gilmore, "The Disciplined Church," *Now*, vol. 3 (Winter, 1973), p. 11.

[6] Champlin Burrage, *The Church Covenant Idea* (Philadelphia: American Baptist Publication Society, 1904), p. 219.

[7] William L. Hendricks, "The Church Covenant: Is It Accurate? Is It Adequate?" *The Baptist Program*, vol. 37 (February, 1961), p. 29.

[8] Allen W. Graves, *A Church at Work* (Nashville: Convention Press, 1972), p. 18.

[9] Robert H. Zbinden, personal letter, March 16, 1973.

[10] Deweese, *op. cit.*, p. 211.

[11] Maring and Hudson, *op. cit.*, p. 73.

[12] Minutes, First Baptist Church of Boston, September, 1682.

[13] Gaines S. Dobbins, *The Churchbook: A Treasury of Materials and Methods* (Nashville: Broadman Press, 1951), p. 5.

[14] Cf. Adam Taylor, *The History of the English General Baptists* (London: T. Bore, 1818), vol. 1, p. 411.

[15] Morgan Edwards, *The Customs of Primitive Churches* (n.p.: n.n., 1774), pp. 5, 67, 77.

[16] Minutes, First Baptist Church of Boston, March, 1665.

[17] Minutes, Middleborough Separate Baptist Church, January, 1756.

[18] Edwards, op. cit., p. 5.

[19] David Thomas, *The Virginian Baptist* (Baltimore: Enoch Story, 1774), pp. 25-26.

[20] William L. Lumpkin, *Baptist Confessions of Faith*, rev. ed. (Valley Forge: Judson Press, 1969), p. 365.

[21] *Annuals*, Southern Baptist Convention, 1925, p. 73; 1963, p. 275.

[22] Maring and Hudson, *op. cit.*, p. 62.

[23] Edwards, *op. cit.*, pp. 4-5; Thomas, *op. cit.*, pp. 26-27.

[24] A. F. Spalding, *The Centennial Discourse on the One Hundredth Anniversary of the First Baptist Church, Warren, R. I., November 15, 1864* (Providence: Knowles, Anthony & Co., 1865), p. 14.

[25] Isaac Backus, *A History of New England: With Particular Reference to the Denomination of Christians Called Baptists*, ed. David Weston, 2d ed. (Newton, Mass.: Backus Memorial Society, 1871), vol. 2, p. 117.

[26] Maring and Hudson, *op. cit.*, p. 73.

[27] Augustine S. Carman, *The Covenant and the Covenant Meeting* (Philadelphia: American Baptist Publication Society, 1898), pp. 28-31.

[28] *Ibid.*, pp. 27, 39.

[29] Edward T. Hiscox, *The New Directory for Baptist Churches* (Philadelphia: American Baptist Publication Society, 1894), p. 249.

[30] Norman H. Maring, *Baptists in New Jersey: A Study in Transition* (Valley Forge: Judson Press, 1964), p. 18.

[31] Henry Melville King, *Rev. John Myles and the Founding of the First Baptist Church in Massachusetts* (Providence, R. I.: Preston & Rounds Co., 1905), pp. 53-54.

[32] Leon McBeth, *The First Baptist Church of Dallas: Centennial History, 1868-1968* (Grand Rapids: The Zondervan Corporation, 1968), p. 245.

Chapter 3

[1] E. Glenn Hinson, "Baptism in the Early Church History," *Review and Expositor*, vol. 65, no. 1 (Winter, 1968), p. 30.

[2] Norman H. Maring and Winthrop S. Hudson, *A Baptist Manual of Polity and Practice* (Valley Forge: Judson Press, 1963), p. 74.

[3] Hippolytus of Rome, *The Treatise on the Apostolic Tradition*, ed. Gregory Dix (London: SPCK, 1968), part 2, section 17.

[4] R. A. Barclay, "New Testament Baptism an External or Internal Rite,"

Initiation, ed. C. J. Bleeker, Studies in the History of Religions, vol. 10 (Leiden: E. J. Brill, 1965), p. 178.

[5] Hinson, *op. cit.,* p. 26.

[6] Paul W. Harkins, trans. and ed., *St. John Chrysostom: Baptismal Instructions,* Ancient Christian Writers (Westminster, Md.: Newman Press, 1963), vol. 31, p. 63.

[7] B. J. Kidd, ed., *Documents Illustrative of the History of the Church* (London: SPCK, 1941), vol. 3, p. 58.

[8] Franklin Hamlin Littell, *The Anabaptist View of the Church,* 2d ed. (Boston: Starr King Press, 1958), p. 85.

[9] Gunnar Westin and Torsten Bergsten, eds., *Balthasar Hübmaier: Schriften,* Quellen zur Geschichte der Taufer, Band IX (Heidelberg: Gutersloher Verlagshaus Gerd Mohn, 1962), pp. 349-350.

[10] W. T. Whitley, ed., *The Works of John Smyth, Fellow of Christ's College, 1594-8* (Cambridge: University Press, 1915), vol. 2, p. 645.

[11] Henry D'Anvers, *A Treatise of Baptism* (London: Elephant and Castle, 1674), p. 216.

[12] John Taylor, *A History of Ten Baptist Churches of Which the Author Has Been Alternately a Member* (Cincinnati: Art Guild Reprints, 1968 [originally 1823]), pp. 6-7.

[13] James William Cox, "Baptism in the Worship Service," *Review and Expositor,* vol. 65, no. 1 (Winter, 1968), p. 53.

[14] Dale Moody, "Baptism" (undated mimeographed essay), pp. 1-7.

[15] *Ibid.,* p. 6.

[16] Maring and Hudson, *op. cit.,* p. 72.

[17] Frank Stagg, "The Lord's Supper in the New Testament," *Review and Expositor,* vol. 66, no. 1 (Winter, 1969), p. 13.

[18] *Ibid.,* pp. 12-13.

[19] G. E. Mendenhall, "Covenant," *The Interpreter's Dictionary of the Bible* (Nashville: Abingdon Press, 1962), vol. 1, p. 722.

[20] Maurice Goguel, *L'euchariste des Origines a Justin Martyr* (Paris: Librairie Fischbacher, 1910), p. 90.

[21] Hippolytus, *op. cit.,* p. 40.

[22] James Cooper and Arthur John Maclean, trans. and eds., *The Testament of Our Lord* (Edinburgh: T. & T. Clark, 1902), p. 128.

[23] Westin and Bergsten, *op. cit.,* pp. 361-362.

[24] Robert A. Macoskey, "The Contemporary Relevance of Balthasar Hübmaier's Concept of the Church," *Foundations,* vol. 6, no. 2 (April, 1963), p. 116.

[25] Charles W. Deweese, "The Origin, Development, and Use of Church Covenants in Baptist History" (unpublished Ph.D. dissertation, Southern Baptist Theological Seminary, 1973), p. 347.

[26] Dale Moody, "The Lord's Supper" (undated mimeographed essay), pp. 5-6.

[27] "Minutes from Olde Pennepack Record Books," *The Chronicle,* vol. 1, no. 3 (July, 1938), p. 126.

[28] Minutes, First Baptist Church of Philadelphia, December 10, 1763.

[29] Morgan Edwards, *The Customs of Primitive Churches* (n.p.: n.n., 1774), pp. 40-41.

[30] Maring and Hudson, *op. cit.*, p. 141.

[31] Stagg, *op. cit.*, p. 14.

[32] E. Glenn Hinson, "The Lord's Supper in Early Church History," *Review and Expositor*, vol. 66, no. 1 (Winter, 1969), p. 24.

[33] C. W. Bess, "New Approach to an Old Ordinance," *The Baptist Program*, August, 1974, p. 24.

Chapter 4

[1] James Leo Garrett, Jr., *Baptist Church Discipline* (Nashville: Broadman Press, 1962), p. 23.

[2] Dietrich Bonhoeffer, *The Cost of Discipleship*, rev. ed. (New York: Macmillan, Inc., 1963), p. 260.

[3] Findley B. Edge, *A Quest for Vitality in Religion* (Nashville: Broadman Press, 1963), p. 223.

[4] Norman H. Maring and Winthrop S. Hudson, *A Baptist Manual of Polity and Practice* (Valley Forge: Judson Press, 1963), pp. 43-44.

[5] J. Herbert Gilmore, Jr., "The Disciplined Church," *Now*, vol. 3 (Winter, 1973), p. 9.

[6] Edge, *op. cit.*, pp. 226-227.

[7] See Garrett, *op. cit.*, p. 3.

[8] Theodor H. Gaster, trans. and ed., *The Dead Sea Scriptures* (Garden City, N.Y.: Doubleday and Company, Inc., 1956), pp. 47-48, 51-55.

[9] Garrett, *op. cit.*, p. 9.

[10] Lowell Hubert Zuck, Abstract of "Anabaptist Revolution Through the Covenant in Sixteenth Century Continental Protestantism" (unpublished Ph.D. dissertation), in *Dissertation Abstracts*, 29:1289-A, October, 1968.

[11] W. T. Whitley, ed., *The Church Books of Ford or Cuddington and Amersham in the County of Bucks* (London: Kingsgate Press, 1912), pp. 202-203.

[12] Elias Keach, *The Glory and Ornament of a True Gospel-Constituted Church* (London: [n.n.], 1697), p. 72.

[13] Morgan Edwards, "History of the Baptists in Delaware," *The Pennsylvania Magazine of History and Biography*, vol. 9 (1885), p. 52.

[14] See, e.g., *Records of the Welsh Tract Baptist Meeting, Pencader Hundred, New Castle County, Delaware, 1701 to 1828*, I, Papers of the Historical Society of Delaware, vol. 42 (Wilmington: Historical Society of Delaware, 1904), p. 30.

[15] See Garrett, *op. cit.*, pp. 13-15, for a good discussion of such treatises and confessions among the early English Baptists.

[16] William L. Lumpkin, *Baptist Confessions of Faith*, rev. ed. (Valley Forge: Judson Press, 1969), p. 358.

[17] Edwin C. Dargan, *Ecclesiology: A Study of the Churches* (Louisville: Charles T. Dearing, 1897), p. 122.

[18] William Warren Sweet, *The Story of Religion in America*, rev. ed. (New York: Harper & Row, Publishers, 1950), pp. 332, 345, 372.

[19] Theodore Gerald Soares, *A Baptist Manual: The Polity of the Baptist Churches and of the Denominational Organizations* (Philadelphia: American Baptist Publication Society, 1911), p. 41.

[20] Z. T. Cody, *History of the Mays Lick Baptist Church* (Maysville, Ky.: G. W. Oldham, 1890), p. 3.

[21] Minutes, New Liberty Baptist Church, Gallatin County, Kentucky, October, 1821.

[22] James Edward Humphrey, "Baptist Discipline in Kentucky, 1781-1960" (unpublished Ph.D. dissertation, Southern Baptist Theological Seminary, 1959), pp. 104-105.

[23] Charles W. Deweese, "Disciplinary Procedures in Frontier Baptist Churches in Kentucky," *Baptist History and Heritage*, vol. 8, no. 4 (October, 1973), pp. 197-198.

[24] William Crowell, *The Church Member's Manual of Ecclesiastical Principles, Doctrine, and Discipline*, rev. ed. (Boston: Gould and Lincoln, 1854), p. 72.

[25] Gilmore, *op. cit.*, pp. 9-11.

[26] Garrett, *op. cit.*, p. 25.

[27] *Ibid.*

[28] William L. Hendricks, "The Church Covenant: Is It Accurate? Is It Adequate?" *The Baptist Program*, vol. 37 (February, 1961), p. 27.

Chapter 5

[1] William L. Lumpkin, *Baptist Confessions of Faith*, rev. ed. (Valley Forge: Judson Press, 1969), p. 398.

[2] "Handbook Issue," *The Quarterly Review*, vol. 36 (July, 1976), p. 7.

[3] *Ibid.*, p. 21.

[4] Cecil E. Sherman, "The Billy Graham Crusade," *The Church Highlights*, January 28, 1977, pp. 1-2.

[5] Norman H. Maring and Winthrop S. Hudson, *A Baptist Manual of Polity and Practice* (Valley Forge: Judson Press, 1963), p. 30.

[6] J. Newton Brown, *The Baptist Church Manual* (Philadelphia: American Baptist Publication Society, 1853), p. 23.

[7] "Covenant of a Church," *Free Baptist Encyclopaedia*, 1889, pp. 138-139.

[8] William Lewis Burdick and Corliss Fitz Randolph, eds., *A Manual of Seventh Day Baptist Church Procedure*, rev. ed. (Plainfield, N.J.: American Sabbath Tract Society, 1926), p. 39.

[9] *Doctrines and Usages of General Baptists and Worker's Handbook*, rev. ed. (Poplar Bluff, Mo.: General Baptist Press, 1949), p. 9.

[10] An excellent introduction to this subject is the article by Roland A. Leavell,

"Evangelism," *Encyclopedia of Southern Baptists* (Nashville: Broadman Press, 1958), vol. 1, pp. 407-419.

[11] The pamphlet "Baptists," available for 10¢ from the Historical Commission, SBC. 127 9th Ave., N., Nashville, TN 37234, is an excellent 16-page resumé of Baptist history. See also *The Story of American Baptists* by Warren Mild, Literature Service LS 15-430, Judson Book Store, Valley Forge, Pennsylvania.

[12] *Southern Baptist Handbook* (Nashville: Sunday School Board, Southern Baptist Convention, 1925), pp. 193-194.

[13] Brooks Hays and John E. Steely, *The Baptist Way of Life* (Englewood Cliffs, N.J.: Prentice-Hall, Inc., 1963), pp. 127-128.

[14] W. L. Muncy, Jr., *A History of Evangelism in the United States* (Kansas City, Kans.: Central Seminary Press, 1945), p. 57.

[15] G. W. Paschal, "Morgan Edwards' Materials Towards a History of the Baptists in the Province of North Carolina," *The North Carolina Historical Review*, vol. 7 (July, 1930), p. 384.

[16] *Ibid.*, p. 385.

[17] William Warren Sweet, *The Story of Religions in America* (New York: Harper & Row, Publishers, 1930), p 220.

[18] Wesley M. Gewehr, *The Great Awakening in Virginia, 1740-1790* (Durham, N.C.: Duke University Press, 1930), p. 176.

Chapter 6

[1] James Leo Garrett, Jr., *Baptist Church Discipline* (Nashville: Broadman Press, 1962), p. 23.

[2] Elton Trueblood, "The Church in the Future," *Catalyst*, vol. 8, no. 2, cited by Albert McClellan, "Integrative Review of Factors and Trends Affecting Program and Product Development" (mimeographed, 1977).

[3] An excellent example is Clyde Reid's *Groups Alive—Church Alive* (New York: Harper & Row, Publishers, 1969). See especially pp. 41-42.

[4] C. E. B. Cranfield, "Diakonia in the New Testament," *Service in Christ: Essays Presented to Karl Barth on His 80th Birthday*, ed. James I. McCord and T. H. L. Parker (London: The Epworth Press, 1966), p. 45.

[5] M. H. Shepherd, "Deacon," *The Interpreter's Dictionary of the Bible*, (Nashville: Abingdon Press, 1962), vol. 1, p. 786.

[6] William L. Lumpkin, *Baptist Confessions of Faith*, rev. ed. (Valley Forge: Judson Press, 1969), pp. 121-122.

[7] Edward Bean Underhill, *The Records of a Church of Christ Meeting in Broadmead, Bristol, 1640-1687* (London: J. Haddon, 1847), pp. 72, 195, 396-398.

[8] Morgan Edwards, "Materials Towards a History of the Baptists in the Province of Virginia," 1772, pp. 56-84.

[9] G. W. Paschall, "Morgan Edwards' Materials Towards a History of the Baptist in the Province of North Carolina [1772]," *The North Carolina Historical Review*, vol. 7 (July, 1930), pp. 384-389.

[10] Morgan Edwards, "Materials Towards a History of the Baptists in the Province of South Carolina," 1772, p. 48.

[11] Morgan Edwards, *The Customs of Primitive Churches* (n.p.: n.n., 1774), p. 43.

[12] For more details on deaconess developments, see Charles W. Deweese, "Deaconesses in Baptist History: A Preliminary Study," *Baptist History and Heritage*, vol. 12, no. 1 (January, 1977), pp. 52-57.

[13] Donald F. Thomas, *The Deacon in a Changing Church* (Valley Forge: Judson Press, 1969), p. 114.

[14] W. T. Whitley, ed., *The Church Books of Ford or Cuddington and Amersham in the County of Bucks* (London: Kingsgate Press, 1912), p. 203.

[15] Minutes, First Baptist Church of Boston, September 13, 1685.

[16] Edward Bean Underhill, ed., *Records of the Churches of Christ Gathered at Fenstanton, Warboys, and Hexham, 1644-1720* (London: Haddon, Brothers, and Co., 1854), pp. 18-19.

[17] For a fuller treatment of this subject, see Charles W. Deweese, "The Functions of Deacons in Early Church History," *The Deacon*, vol. 5, no. 3 (April–June, 1975), pp. 23-25.

[18] *Records of the Welsh Tract Baptist Meeting*, vol. 2 (Wilmington, Del.: Historical Society of Delaware, 1904), p. 8.

[19] Stephen Wright, comp., *History of the Shaftsbury Association from 1781 to 1853* (Troy, N.Y.: A. G. Johnson, 1853), p. 98.

[20] R. B. C. Howell, *The Deaconship* (Philadelphia: American Baptist Publication Society, 1846), pp. 122-123.

[21] J. B. McMinn, "Deacon," *Encyclopedia of Southern Baptists* (Nashville: Broadman Press, 1958), vol. 1, p. 352.

[22] Eusebius, *Church History*, VII.xxi.7-8; *The Nicene and Post-Nicene Fathers*, second series, vol. 1, p. 307.

[23] E. K. Love, *History of the First African Baptist Church* (Savannah: Morning News Print, 1888), p. 163.

[24] Frank L. Wilkins, *The Diaconate: As It Is and As It Ought to Be* (Philadelphia: American Baptist Publication Society, 1915), pp. 7-8.

Index